HEARTLAND COOKING

BREADS

HEARTLAND COOKING
BREADS

FRANCES TOWNER GIEDT

PHOTOGRAPHS BY
Eleanor Thompson

The Reader's Digest Association, Inc.
Pleasantville, New York/Montreal

A Reader's Digest Book

CONCEIVED AND PRODUCED BY
Miller & O'Shea, Inc.

DESIGNED BY
Lynette Cortez Design

The acknowledgments that appear on page 5 are hereby made a part of this copyright page.

Library of Congress Cataloging in Publication Data
Giedt, Frances Towner.
   Breads / by Frances Towner Giedt : photographs by Eleanor
Thompson.
      p.   cm. — (Heartland cooking)
   Includes index.
   ISBN 0-89577-854-8
   1. Bread.   2. Automatic bread machines.   I. Title.   II. Series.
TX769.G53 1996
641.8'15 — dc20   95-43418

Printed in the United States of America
Second Printing, August 1997

IN MEMORY OF MY PARENTS,
EDITH AND HARRY TOWNER
who instilled in me a love of the land and its bounty

and

TO MEGAN ERIKA
my first grandchild, who began her life
just as we were beginning the photography for this book

ACKNOWLEDGMENTS

IT WAS DURING A LONG DRIVE FROM CONNECTICUT TO TEXAS THAT I BEGAN TO CLEARLY ENVISION THIS book. As the project grew, it reminded me of a tumbleweed, but instead of gathering up fragments of stone and other debris as it crossed the plains, this cookbook project gathered up people, each contributing to the end result in their own talented way.

My heartfelt thanks go to Eleanor Thompson for her stunning photographs and to her assistant, Chris Hobson; to Paul E. Piccuito for his baking and food styling; and to Deborah Slocomb for propping each photo.

A special thanks to Coleen O'Shea and Angela Miller for giving me the opportunity to write about the food of the Midwest; to Lynette Cortez, for her beautiful, creative design of this book; and to Kathy Knapp, whose skillful talent in turning a phrase contributed much to the book.

Many thanks to the following shops and stores who generously let us borrow extensively from their shelves for the photography of the recipes: Anthropology, Westport, CT; The Complete Kitchen, Darien, CT; Eddie Bauer, Home Design; The Forgotten Garden, Wilton, CT; Francis Hill Antiques, Wilton, CT; Gilbertie's Herb Farm, Westport, CT; Hoagland's, Greenwich, CT; L.C.R., Westport, CT; Metropolitan Museum Store, Stamford, CT; Pier 1 Imports; Pottery Barn; Simon Pearce, Westport, CT; Villeroy & Boch; Wayside Exchange & Antiques, Wilton, CT; Williams-Sonoma.

Thanks also to The Hitachi Corporation, Zojirushi American Corporation, Kitchen Aid Portable Appliances, and Maytag Dairy Farms for their contributions.

My love and appreciation to my husband David for his encouragement and support, and for his untiring care of our home in Texas during my long absence while we were photographing this Heartland book.

C O N T

BUTTERS, SPREADS, AND JAMS

ENTS

QUICK BREADS 93

SOURCES AND INDEX 142

AMERICA'S VAST HEARTLAND, STRETCHING FROM THE ALLEGHENIES TO THE ROCKIES and from the Canadian border south to the Red River that divides Oklahoma and Texas, is composed of thirteen states—Kansas, Illinois, Indiana, Iowa, Michigan, Minnesota, Missouri, Nebraska, North Dakota, Ohio, Oklahoma, South Dakota, and Wisconsin. The cuisine of this fertile land is grounded in a hearty and healthy love of food.

I'm proud to say I'm from Kansas. My grandfather immigrated to southcentral Kansas, 56 miles southwest of Wichita, in the late-1800's, and with 160 acres of land began a family history of wheat farming. My mother was born and raised on that farm, and since there were no boys in the family, she was expected to work the fields, clearing the rich red earth of rocks, and pulling the plow with the help of one mare to plant the wheat.

Like other farmers, my grandparents planted a huge kitchen garden; had a small herd of cows for meat, milk, and freshly churned butter; raised pigs for hams, bacon, and sausages; and kept a large flock of **INTRO** chickens for Sunday dinners and a steady supply of fresh eggs. At every meal the table was laden with the results of their labor; fresh food was in abundance.

I first learned to cook in my mother's kitchen. Some of my fondest memories were watching her bake bread. I seldom saw her use a recipe and she rarely measured the ingredients, but her dinner rolls were light as a feather, her muffins were never riddled with tunnels, her biscuits were tender and flaky, and her yeast bread was the ultimate comfort food.

In this book, I offer a collection of bread recipes that reflect the good cookery of the Heartland. Many of these recipes are updated versions of my mother's or other family members' recipes. I developed others in my kitchen, taking into account the indigenous foods of the many ethnic groups that make up today's Heartland.

These bread recipes are packed with flavor and showcase the vast Heartland culinary assets: abundant cultivated grain crops, garden fresh vegetables, orchard fruits, and culinary delicacies such as luscious berries, dried cherries, tart persimmons, wild rice, and native black walnuts.

Here, you'll find mouth-watering recipes for yeast breads and quick breads that connect the Heartland past with the modern foodstyles of today, with a special section geared for use in automatic bread making machines.

The recipes in this book provide easy-to-understand instructions so that even if you have never baked a loaf of bread, cut out a biscuit, or mixed a muffin, you can now experience the joy of baking bread.

AN ARRAY OF GRAINS In earlier times, white flour made from wheat was the only flour available. When the wheat crop failed, the pioneer housewives ground flour from oats, corn, buckwheat, and other grains in their coffee mills.

DUCTION

Fortunately, a wide variety of flours and grains are now available at the supermarket and natural food store. These recipes call for the familiar—wheat, corn, oats, and rye— as well as barley, cracked wheat, gluten flour, millet, brown rice, whole wheat, and wild rice. Unbleached all-purpose or unbleached bread flour make the best choice for making bread. Unbleached flour, allowed to whiten and age naturally, even with its nutrient-rich bran and germ removed, is higher in nutritive value, flavor, and rising ability than bleached flour. This natural aging process intensifies the gluten in the flour, making a more elastic or springier dough. Unbleached all-purpose flour is available in the flour section of your local supermarket.

OTHER BREAD INGREDIENTS Leaveners produce the carbon dioxide gas that lightens doughs and batters. In yeast breads, yeast is the leavening. Quick breads rely on a chemical leavening agent such as baking powder and/or baking soda. In popovers, the steam formed as the thin batter bakes is the leavening.

Liquids dissolve and activate the yeast and other leavening agents and develop the gluten structure of the flour. These recipes use a variety of liquids (water, milk, dry nonfat milk, cream, fruit juices, evaporated milk, fresh buttermilk, and sour cream), each imparting a different flavor and texture to the finished bread.

Sweetenings such as sugar, brown sugar, honey, maple syrup, and molasses provide food for the yeast, give tenderness to the bread, help brown the crust while the bread is baking, and contribute their flavor and color to the breads.

Fats give bread a tender, moist texture and a rich flavor. They also help to keep the bread fresh once it's baked. These recipes call for fats such as butter, olive oil, canola oil, milk, eggs, and cheese.

Salt is a flavor enhancer. It can be omitted if you are on a salt-restricted diet, but the lack of salt will be quite noticeable. Coarse salt is sprinkled on top of some of the loaves for decoration.

TOOLS AND EQUIPMENT Bread making requires very little equipment: a 12-cup mixing bowl, measuring cups and spoons, a heavy wooden spoon, and baking pans. A thermometer will correctly measure the temperature of water or milk for dissolving the yeast.

For mixing the dough, an electric mixer with a paddle attachment or dough hook will make light work of the mixing and kneading, but you can always mix and knead by hand. A food processor is efficient for mixing many of the doughs and batters. An automatic bread making machine (there are many excellent models available) is necessary for the bread machine recipes. This Japanese invention is nothing short of magic for producing old-fashioned loaves with little work.

For shaping and glazing, you'll need a rolling pin, a pastry or bread board, a razor blade or sharp serrated knife, a biscuit cutter, and a clean pastry brush.

For baking, aluminum pans are lightweight and the best conductor of heat. Buy the best you can afford, preferably a grade suitable for professional bakers. Clay and stainless steel pans are also good heat conductors and will produce crisp crusts. Glass and black-tinned pans brown bread more quickly; so reduce oven heat by 25°.

BAKING AT HIGH ALTITUDES
Altitudes over 3,000 feet affect bread baking

methods because the atmosphere is drier due to lower air pressure. The following is a general guide:

Yeast: For every tablespoon or package, *decrease* by ½ teaspoon at elevations above 3,000 feet.

Baking powder and baking soda: For each teaspoon, *decrease* by ⅛ teaspoon at more than 3,000 feet and by ¼ teaspoon at levels of 5,000 feet and above.

Liquids: For each cup, *increase* by 1 tablespoon at more than 3,000 feet, by 2 to 3 tablespoons at 5,000 feet, and by 3 to 4 tablespoons at 6,500 feet and above.

Sweetenings: For each cup, *decrease* by 1 tablespoon at more than 3,000 feet, by 2 tablespoons at 5,000 feet, and by 3 tablespoons at 6,500 feet and above.

Flour: For each cup, *increase* by 1 tablespoon at more than 3,000 feet, by 2 tablespoons at 5,000 feet, and by 3 tablespoons at 6,500 feet and above.

METRIC CONVERSION CHART

LIQUID AND DRY MEASURE EQUIVALENTS

Customary	Metric
¼ teaspoon	1.25 milliliters
½ teaspoon	2.5 milliliters
1 teaspoon	5 milliliters
1 tablespoon	15 milliliters
1 fluid ounce	30 milliliters
¼ cup	60 milliliters
⅓ cup	80 milliliters
½ cup	120 milliliters
1 cup	240 milliliters
1 pint (2 cups)	480 milliliters
1 quart (4 cups; 32 ounces)	960 milliliters (.96 liter)
1 gallon (4 quarts)	3.84 liters
1 ounce (by weight)	28.35 grams
¼ pound (4 ounces)	114 grams
1 pound (16 ounces)	454 grams
2.2 pounds	1 kilogram (1,000 grams)

TEMPERATURE EQUIVALENTS

Description	°Fahrenheit	°Celsius
Cool	200	90
Very slow	250	120
Slow	300-325	150-160
Moderately slow	325-350	160-180
Moderate	350-375	180-190
Moderately hot	375-400	190-200
Hot	400-450	200-230
Very hot	450-500	230-260

COOKING AND BAKING EQUIVALENTS

Bakeware	Customary	Metric
Round Pan	8 x 1½ inches	20 x 4 cm
	9 x 1½ inches	23 x 4 cm
	10 x 1½ inches	25 x 4 cm
Square Pan	8 x 8 x 2 inches	20 x 20 x 5 cm
	9 x 9 x 2 inches	23 x 23 x 5 cm
Baking Dishes	7 x 11 x 1½ inches	18 x 28 x 4 cm
	7½ x 12 x 2 inches	19 x 30 x 5 cm
	9 x 13 x 2 inches	23 x 33 x 5 cm
Loaf Pan	8½ x 4½ x 2½ inches	11 x 21 x 6 cm
	9 x 5 x 3 inches	13 x 23 x 8 cm
Muffin Cups	2½ x 1¼ inches	6 x 3 cm
	3 x 1½ inches	8 x 4 cm
Casseroles and Saucepans	1 quart	1 L
	1½ quart	1.5 L
	2 quart	2 L
	2½ quart	2.5 L
	3 quart	3 L
	4 quart	4 L

YEAST BREADS

REAKING INTO A LOAF OF YEAST BREAD that you've made yourself is one of life's most soul-satisfying moments. Nothing smells or tastes better than your own oven-fresh bread.

"Proofing" is the term that describes the process of activating the yeast with a liquid. If using active dry yeast, the yeast and 1 teaspoon of sugar is sprinkled over lukewarm liquid (110°F — about the temperature of a warmed baby bottle) and stirred until the yeast completely dissolves. The other ingredients are added, the dough is allowed to rise until doubled in size, then punched down, and formed into a loaf for a second rising before baking.

Sponge Method: Yeast, sugar, a portion of the total liquid, and some of the flour are whisked together and the sponge is allowed to rest at room temperature until bubbly, usually for 1 hour to overnight, depending on the type of bread. After the other ingredients are added, the dough requires two risings before baking: before and after shaping the loaf.

Rapid-Mix Method: A quick one-rise yeast was developed in the 1960s. In this method, part of the flour and all other dry ingredients are mixed with the yeast and activated by hot liquid (120° to 130°F — use an instant-reading thermometer), then mixed to form a creamy batter. The yeast dissolves immediately and the dough is then mixed, kneaded, allowed to rest for a few minutes, formed into a loaf, and allowed to rise before baking. Due to the rapid fermentation of the one-rise yeast, there will be some loss in texture and flavor of the finished bread. For most home bakers, however, any loss in quality is more than made up for by the decreased rising time.

MIXING THE DOUGH

YOU MAY MIX AND KNEAD DOUGH BY HAND, by electric mixer with a paddle attachment or dough hook, or electric food processor. By hand, it takes about 10 minutes to mix and knead the dough; by electric mixer, about 5 to 7 minutes; with a food processor, about 1 minute. Specific directions are given in the recipes.

RISING

I USE A DEEP CROCKERY BOWL OR 4-QUART PLASTIC container for rising dough. Avoid metal bowls since they conduct heat easily and can actually cook the dough if the kitchen is too warm. Grease the container and turn the dough over once to grease the top. A clean cloth or clear plastic wrap makes a good cover.

One of my recipes specifically calls for a cool-rise in the refrigerator. Actually any yeast dough can be refrigerated for 2 to 24 hours. The dough will rise to about 1 inch above the rim of the pan. Return the dough to room temperature (about 20 minutes) while the oven is preheating before shaping into a loaf.

SHAPING AND BAKING

THE SHAPING OF YEAST BREAD TAKES SOME practice, but the main objective is to form a loaf with a smooth top. Pinch all seams together to close. Once the loaf is formed, place the loaf, seam side down, on a lightly greased or parchment-lined baking sheet or in a lightly greased loaf pan.

Prior to baking, loaves are frequently cut with decorative slashes to allow the dough to expand during baking. You can cut patterns that are your personal trademark using a quick motion with a razor blade or sharp serrated knife and cutting no more than ¼-inch deep. Commonly used patterns are an X, cross-hatch, or parallel diagonal slashes.

Place the loaf in a preheated oven on the center to lowest shelf. Leave at least 2 inches between multiple pans for best heat circulation. Technically, the bread is still baking while it's cooling. Unless the recipe specifies differently, it's best to allow the bread to cool in the pan for a few minutes, then on a rack for easier slicing with a serrated bread knife.

FREEZING AND REHEATING

THE FREEZER SECTION OF YOUR REFRIGERATOR will keep bread for up to three months. To freeze yeast bread, wrap whole or pre-sliced, cooled loaves of baked bread in plastic wrap, then aluminum foil or polyethylene freezer bags. Label and date the package. Thaw at room temperature, completely unwrapped, for about 3 hours. To reheat in the oven, rewrap the bread in aluminum foil and place in a preheated 350°F oven for 15 minutes. Sliced bread may be refreshed in a toaster.

APPLE CINNAMON ROLLS

MAKES 9 ROLLS

Some of the world's best-tasting apples come from the Heartland. "You-pick" orchards are commonplace and some enterprising fruit farms offer tree rentals where, for an annual fee, you can pick and take home all the apples grown on your rented tree.

These giant spiraled rolls are dense with apples and cinnamon. Shaped and ready to bake, they only need one rising and since that can be done in the refrigerator, they're ready to be baked right before you want to serve them. If you're having a crowd for breakfast, you can always double the recipe. The baked rolls freeze well.

1 package (¼ ounce) active dry yeast	2 large eggs, slightly beaten
¼ cup granulated sugar	¾ cup firmly packed light brown sugar
¼ cup warm spring water, about 110°F	½ cup finely chopped pecans
7 tablespoons butter, at room temperature	1 cup peeled, cored, and finely chopped tart apples, such as Granny Smith, Ida Red, or Prairie Spy
¼ cup whole milk	
¼ teaspoon salt	
2 to 2¼ cups unbleached all-purpose flour	¾ teaspoon ground cinnamon

PREP TIME:
45 MIN + 1½ HR
FOR RISING OR
16–18 HR
REFRIGERATOR
RISING

BAKE TIME:
30 MIN

1. In a small bowl, sprinkle yeast and 1 teaspoon of the granulated sugar over warm spring water and stir until yeast completely dissolves. Let stand until foamy, about 5 minutes.

2. In a large mixing bowl, combine 3 tablespoons butter, milk, the remaining granulated sugar, and the salt. Gradually stir in 1 cup of the flour, the eggs, and yeast mixture. Mix well. Stir in another cup of the flour to make a soft dough. Turn out onto a lightly floured work surface and knead until smooth and elastic, about 10 minutes, adding up to ¼ cup additional flour, 1 tablespoon at a time, as needed to keep dough from sticking. Let dough rest for 15 minutes.

3. Meanwhile, in a small bowl, combine the remaining 4 tablespoons butter and ½ cup of the brown sugar. Spread mixture in a well oiled 9-inch square metal baking pan. Top evenly with pecans.

4. Roll out dough to form a 10- by 12-inch rectangle. In a small bowl, combine apples, the remaining ¼ cup brown sugar, and cinnamon. Place apple mixture on dough, spreading filling to ¼ inch from the edges.

5. Working from the 12-inch side, roll up dough tightly to enclose filling. Pinch seams to seal. With a sharp knife, cut roll into 9 equal pieces.

6. Place rolls, cut side down, on top of pecans. Cover with plastic wrap and let rise in a warm place until doubled in bulk, about 1½ hours (or for 16 to 18 hours in a refrigerator).

7. If rolls have been refrigerated, let stand at room temperature for 20 minutes before baking. When ready to bake, preheat oven to 350°F. Bake until golden brown, about 30 minutes. Invert immediately onto a serving platter. Let pan remain briefly on rolls so the topping can drizzle down. Let cool at least 10 minutes before serving.

1 roll : 334 calories, 6 g protein, 15 g total fat (6.5 g saturated), 45 g carbohydrates, 174 mg sodium, 72 mg cholesterol, 2 g dietary fiber

APRICOT THREE-GRAIN BREAD

MAKES 2 LOAVES (12 SLICES EACH)

Saffron is the dried stigma of a small purple crocus. Since each crocus only provides three stigmas and the stigmas must be hand-picked, production of saffron is labor intensive, making it the world's most expensive spice. Fortunately a little saffron goes a long way to add its distinctive flavor and yellow color.

1½ cups chopped dried apricots (8 ounces)
  Boiling water
¼ teaspoon saffron threads
½ cup milk
3½ to 4½ cups unbleached all-purpose flour
1½ teaspoons salt
2 packages (¼ ounce each) rapid-rise yeast

1¼ cups spring water
½ cup (1 stick) butter
¼ cup honey
2 large eggs, slightly beaten
2 cups stone-ground whole wheat flour
1 cup regular or quick rolled oats, uncooked
1 cup raw, hulled sunflower seeds

1. Put apricots in a small saucepan and add boiling water to cover. Let stand for 5 minutes. Drain well. Bring saffron threads and milk to a simmer in a small saucepan. Let cool.
2. Set aside 1 cup of the all-purpose flour. In a large bowl, combine 2½ cups of the all-purpose flour, the salt, and yeast. In a saucepan, heat spring water and butter until butter begins to melt and mixture reaches 120°F.
3. **To knead with a dough hook,** using medium speed of mixer, gradually beat the water mixture into the flour mixture. Continue beating for 2 minutes. Add the honey, eggs, milk mixture, and the whole wheat flour; beat another 2 minutes. Add the oats, sunflower seeds, and another 1 cup all-purpose flour. Continue to beat on medium speed until dough is no longer sticky and cleanly pulls away from the bowl, 5 to 7 minutes, adding up to 1 cup of the reserved flour, 1 tablespoon at a time, as needed to keep dough from sticking. Turn dough out onto a lightly floured work surface. Cover with a towel and let dough rest for 15 minutes.

To knead by hand, using a heavy wooden spoon, gradually beat the water mixture into the flour mixture. Add the honey, eggs, milk mixture, and the whole wheat flour; beat well. Gradually add the oats, sunflower seeds, and another 1 cup all-purpose flour. Turn dough out onto a lightly floured work surface and knead until smooth and elastic, about 10 minutes, adding up to 1 cup of the reserved flour, 1 tablespoon at a time, as needed to keep dough from sticking. Cover with a towel and let dough rest for 15 minutes.
4. Grease two 9 x 5 x 3-inch loaf pans. Pat dough into a 1-inch thick rectangle. Place apricots on top of half of the dough; fold dough over fruit. Lightly knead to incorporate apricots evenly into the dough. Divide dough in half and shape each portion into a loaf. Place loaves seam side down in prepared pans. Cover and let rise in a warm place until doubled in bulk, about 45 minutes.
5. Preheat oven to 375°F. Bake until golden brown, 40 to 45 minutes. Cool in pans for 5 minutes. Remove from pans and cool on a rack.

PREP TIME: 35 MIN + 45 MIN FOR RISING
BAKE TIME: 40–45 MIN

1 slice: 235 calories, 7 g protein, 8 g total fat (3.0 g saturated), 36 g carbohydrates, 183 mg sodium, 29 mg cholesterol, 3 g dietary fiber

BUBBLE BREAD

MAKES 1 RING (16 SERVINGS)

There are many versions of this richly glazed bread, made by layering balls of dough in a tube pan. The balls break off into individual rolls for serving.

A friend told me she makes Bubble Bread with Grand Marnier for Christmas brunch. I added it as a festive touch to my family's recipe. ▶

BUBBLE BREAD *(see previous page for photo and notes)*

3½ to 4½ cups unbleached all-purpose flour
¼ cup granulated sugar
1 package (¼ ounce) rapid-rise dry yeast
1 teaspoon salt
1 cup whole milk, scalded and cooled
  to lukewarm
¼ cup spring water
½ cup (1 stick) butter, at room temperature

1 large egg, slightly beaten
½ cup firmly packed light brown sugar
1 teaspoon ground cinnamon
½ teaspoon ground nutmeg
¼ cup Grand Marnier or other orange liqueur
1 tablespoon grated orange rind
½ cup chopped walnuts

**PREP TIME:
40 MIN +
45 MIN
FOR RISING

BAKE TIME:
40–45 MIN**

1. Set aside 1 cup of the flour. In a large bowl, combine 1 cup flour, granulated sugar, yeast, and salt. In a small saucepan, heat milk, water, and ¼ cup of the butter until butter begins to melt and mixture reaches 120°F. Using medium speed of an electric mixer, gradually beat the milk mixture into the flour mixture. Continue beating for 2 minutes. Add the egg and another cup of the flour; beat another 2 minutes.

2. **To knead with a dough hook,** gradually add 1½ cups of the flour, ½ cup at a time, until mixture forms a stiff dough. Continue to beat on medium speed until dough is springy and cleanly pulls away from the bowl, 5 to 7 minutes, adding up to 1 cup of the reserved flour, 1 tablespoon at a time, as needed to keep dough from sticking. Cover and let dough rest for 15 minutes.

To knead by hand, beating with a wooden spoon, gradually add 1½ cups of the flour, ½ cup at a time, until mixture forms a stiff dough. Turn dough onto a lightly floured work surface and knead by hand until smooth and elastic, about 10 minutes, adding up to 1 cup of the reserved flour, 1 tablespoon at a time, as needed to keep dough from sticking. Cover and let dough rest for 15 minutes.

3. Butter a 9-inch tube or Bundt pan. Pinch off pieces of dough and, with your fingertips, shape each piece into a smooth ball about 1½ inches in diameter. (You will have about 16 balls.) Place one layer of balls about ½ inch apart in prepared pan.

4. In a small saucepan, melt the remaining ¼ cup butter. Stir in the brown sugar, cinnamon, nutmeg, Grand Marnier, and grated orange rind. Spoon ⅓ of the mixture over the balls of dough in the pan. Sprinkle with ⅓ of the walnuts. Repeat, arranging two more layers, placing the balls over the spaces in the layer below and topping each layer with the butter mixture and walnuts. Cover and let rise in a warm place until doubled in bulk, about 45 minutes.

5. Preheat oven to 350°F. Bake for 40 to 45 minutes, until golden brown. Remove from oven and cool in pan for 10 minutes before inverting onto a serving plate or board. Serve warm.

1 serving: 247 calories, 5 g protein, 9 g total fat (4.3 g saturated), 35 g carbohydrates, 207 mg sodium, 31 mg cholesterol, 1 g dietary fiber

MICROWAVE CRANBERRY-STRAWBERRY CONSERVE

MAKES 1 PINT

PREP TIME: 5 MIN • COOK TIME: 15 MIN

2 cups cranberries, rinsed, drained, and picked over
1 cup halved hulled strawberries
2 cups sugar
2 tablespoons fresh lemon juice
1 teaspoon grated lemon rind

1. Combine all ingredients in a covered 4-quart microwave-safe bowl.

2. Cook, covered, at HIGH power (650 to 700 watts) for 15 minutes, stirring well every 2 to 3 minutes.

3. Allow conserve to cool slightly. Transfer to sterilized jars and refrigerate for up to 1 week. Or, transfer to plastic freezer containers and freeze for up to 3 months. (The conserve will thicken as it chills.)

1 tablespoon: 53 calories, 0 protein, 0 total fat, 14 g carbohydrates, 0 sodium, 0 cholesterol, 0 dietary fiber

CINNAMON PECAN CRISPS

MAKES 24 CRISPS

Midwesterners love pecans — native pecans grow wild in the southwestern part of Missouri where bags of cracked nuts are sold at roadside stands, farmers' markets, and mail-order (see Sources, page 142). Moister than cultivated Southern pecans, Missouri pecans are perfect for these giant cinnamon rolls.

A special treat for a late morning brunch, these rolls are similar to the elephant ear pastries sold at the county fairs. Don't expect them to last long after they come out of the oven.

SPONGE

2 packages (¼ ounce each) active dry yeast
2 tablespoons granulated sugar
½ cup warm spring water, about 110°F
1¼ cups warm whole milk, about 110°F
1 cup unbleached all-purpose flour

DOUGH

2 large eggs, slightly beaten
3 tablespoons grated orange rind
¼ cup granulated sugar
1 teaspoon salt

4 to 4 ½ cups unbleached all-purpose flour
6 tablespoons (¾ stick) butter, cut into 6 pieces, at room temperature

FILLING

½ cup (1 stick) butter
1½ cups granulated sugar
½ cup firmly packed light brown sugar
¾ cup finely chopped pecans
2 teaspoons ground cinnamon
1 cup pecan halves

> **PREP TIME:**
> **40 MIN + 30 MIN**
> **RESTING TIME FOR**
> **SPONGE AND 1 ½ HR**
> **FOR RISING**
> **BAKE TIME:**
> **10–12 MIN**

1. **To prepare sponge:** In a large bowl, whisk together yeast, sugar, warm spring water, warm milk, and flour. Cover with plastic wrap and let rise in a warm place until bubbly, about 30 minutes.

2. **To make dough:** After 30 minutes, add eggs, orange rind, sugar, salt, and 1 cup flour to the sponge. Beat until smooth. Add butter, one piece at a time, beating well after each addition. Using a wooden spoon, add another 3 cups of flour, ½ cup at a time, mixing well after each addition. Turn dough out onto a lightly floured work surface and knead by hand until smooth and elastic, about 10 minutes, adding up to ½ cup additional flour, 1 tablespoon at a time, as needed to keep dough from sticking.

3. Place dough in a lightly greased bowl, turning dough over once to coat top. Cover and let rise in a warm place until doubled in bulk, about 1 hour. Punch down dough and knead briefly on a lightly floured work surface to release the air. Divide dough in half and roll out each portion to a 12-inch square.

4. **To make filling:** In a small saucepan, melt ¼ cup butter. Stir in 1 cup granulated sugar, the brown sugar, the finely chopped pecans, and 1 teaspoon of the cinnamon. Divide the mixture and spread on top of the rolled dough pieces to within ¼-inch of the edges. Roll up each piece jelly-roll-fashion and pinch to seal ends. Cut each crosswise into twelve 1-inch pieces. Place cut side down on greased baking sheets at least 3 inches apart. Flatten each piece to about 3 inches in diameter. Cover loosely with plastic wrap and let rise in a warm place for 30 minutes. Using a rolling pin, flatten each piece to about ⅛-inch thickness about 6 inches in diameter. Carefully remove plastic wrap.

5. Preheat oven to 400°F. Melt the remaining ¼ cup butter and combine with the remaining ½ cup sugar, the remaining 1 teaspoon cinnamon, and the pecan halves. Sprinkle over rolls, pressing the mixture into the dough with your fingers. Bake until golden brown, about 10 to 12 minutes. Transfer to racks to cool slightly before serving.

1 crisp: 302 calories, 5 g protein, 13 g total fat (5.1 g saturated), 42 g carbohydrates, 171 mg sodium, 38 mg cholesterol, 2 g dietary fiber

CHRISTMAS CRANBERRY COFFEE WREATH

MAKES 1 WREATH (16 SERVINGS)

My mother made this coffee cake with candied mixed fruit. For the holidays, make it with dried cranberries. Its braided wreath shape shows off the colorful filling and gives the bread a festive appearance. Decorate the wreath with fresh juniper or pine boughs.

Dried cranberries are available in many supermarkets, natural food stores, and by mail-order (see Sources, page 142).

½ cup finely chopped blanched almonds	½ teaspoon ground cardamom
½ cup dried cranberries	¾ cup whole milk
3½ to 4 cups unbleached all-purpose flour	¼ cup spring water
⅓ cup sugar	6 tablespoons (¾ stick) butter, at room temperature
1 package (¼ ounce) rapid-rise yeast	
1 tablespoon grated fresh orange rind	2 large eggs, slightly beaten
1 teaspoon salt	½ teaspoon almond extract

PREP TIME: 40 MIN + 1 HR FOR RISING

BAKE TIME: 20–25 MIN

1. In a small bowl, combine almonds and dried cranberries. Set aside.

2. In a large bowl, combine 1 cup flour, the sugar, yeast, orange rind, salt, and cardamon. In a small saucepan, heat milk, water, and 5 tablespoons of the butter until butter begins to melt and mixture reaches 120°F. Stir the milk mixture into the flour mixture. Stir in the eggs and almond extract.

3. **To knead with a dough hook,** gradually add another 2½ cups of the flour, ½ cup at a time, until mixture forms a stiff dough. Continue to beat on medium speed until dough is springy and cleanly pulls away from the bowl, 5 to 7 minutes, adding up to ½ cup additional flour, 1 tablespoon at a time, as needed to keep dough from sticking. Turn dough onto a lightly floured work surface.

To knead by hand, beating with a wooden spoon, gradually add another 2½ cups of the flour, ½ cup at a time, until mixture forms a stiff dough. Turn dough onto a lightly floured work surface and knead by hand until smooth and elastic, about 10 minutes, adding up to ½ cup additional flour, 1 tablespoon at a time, as needed to keep dough from sticking.

4. Pat dough into a rectangle about 1 inch thick. Place almond-cranberry mixture over half of the dough. Fold over the dough and lightly knead until mixture is evenly distributed. Place dough in a lightly greased bowl, turning dough over once to coat top. Cover and let dough rest for 15 minutes.

5. Divide dough into thirds. On a lightly floured work surface, roll each third with your hands, rolling from the center, to form three ropes 20 inches long. Place ropes on a greased baking sheet, crossing at the center. Braid out to each end. Form braid into a 12-inch ring and pinch ends together. Lightly cover and let rise in a warm place until doubled in bulk, about 1 hour.

6. Preheat oven to 375°F. Bake until lightly browned, about 20 to 25 minutes. Melt remaining 1 tablespoon butter and brush over top of wreath. Transfer to a rack to cool.

1 serving: 214 calories, 5 g protein, 8 g total fat (3.4 g saturated), 31 g carbohydrates, 192 mg sodium, 40 mg cholesterol, 2 g dietary fiber

COUNTRY LOAF

MAKES 2 LOAVES (12 SLICES EACH)

Cracked wheat, sprinkled on the loaf just before baking, gives this rustic loaf a nutty flavor and crunchy texture. I can buy cracked wheat at my supermarket, but you may need to look for it at a natural food store.

This recipe calls for a sponge that takes at least 12 hours, so plan to make it the night before. The long fermentation period results in a finely textured bread with a tangy flavor similar to sourdough bread. The recipe makes two loaves — serve one with tonight's dinner; freeze the other for later.

SPONGE

- 2 packages (¼ ounce each) active dry yeast
- 1½ cups warm spring water, about 110°F
- 2 teaspoons sugar
- 2 cups unbleached all-purpose flour

DOUGH

- ½ cup stone-ground whole wheat flour
- 1 cup warm spring water
- 4 to 4½ cups unbleached all-purpose flour
- 2 teaspoons salt
- 1 large egg white beaten with 1 tablespoon water
- ⅓ cup cracked wheat

PREP TIME: 30 MIN + 12 HR RESTING TIME FOR SPONGE AND 2 HR FOR RISING

BAKE TIME: 30–35 MIN

1. Make the sponge at least 12 hours ahead: In a large bowl, sprinkle yeast over ½ cup warm spring water. Stir until yeast dissolves completely. Let stand until foamy, about 5 minutes. Stir in another 1 cup warm water, the sugar, and 2 cups unbleached all-purpose flour. Beat by hand or electric mixer for 1 minute. Cover bowl with plastic wrap and let stand at room temperature for 12 hours.

2. Later that day or the next day, stir the whole wheat flour, 1 cup warm spring water, 4 cups all-purpose flour, and the salt into the sponge mixture. Turn dough out onto a lightly floured work surface and knead by hand until dough is smooth and elastic, about 10 minutes, adding up to ½ cup additional all-purpose flour, 1 tablespoon at a time, as needed to prevent dough from sticking to hands.

3. Place dough in a lightly greased bowl, turning dough over once to coat top. Cover and let rise in a warm place until doubled in bulk, about 1 to 1½ hours.

4. Punch down dough and knead briefly on a lightly floured work surface to release the air. Divide dough into two equal portions and shape each portion into a round loaf, gently pulling top surface under until smooth. Place each loaf on a lightly greased baking sheet. Cover and let rise in a warm place until doubled in bulk, about 1 hour.

5. Preheat oven to 450°F. Brush the top and sides of each loaf with beaten egg white and sprinkle with cracked wheat. Bake for 10 minutes. Reduce heat to 350°F. Loosely cover with aluminum foil and continue to bake for another 20 to 25 minutes, until bread is golden brown and sounds hollow when tapped on the bottom.

1 slice: 138 calories, 4 g protein, 0 g total fat, 29 g carbohydrates, 181 mg sodium, 0 cholesterol, 2 g dietary fiber

DILL BATTER BREAD

MAKES 1 LOAF (12 SERVINGS)

Batter breads are easy to make and require no kneading, just a quick beating with an electric mixer. Dill is a popular herb throughout the Midwest. Even cooks who have a limited spice rack keep a bottle of dried dill weed handy for cooking and baking.

Look for dry buttermilk in the baking goods aisle of your supermarket near the nonfat dry milk, or replace ½ cup of the water with ½ cup fresh cultured low-fat (1.5%) buttermilk.

This is the kind of bread you'll find at Heartland potluck dinners and church suppers.

1 package (¼ ounce) active dry yeast	2 tablespoons butter, at room temperature
2 tablespoons sugar	1 large egg, slightly beaten
1⅓ cups warm spring water, about 110°F	3¼ cups unbleached all-purpose flour
1 teaspoon salt	¼ cup minced onion
2 tablespoons dry buttermilk (or see note, above)	3 tablespoons chopped fresh dill or 1 tablespoon dried dill weed
⅛ teaspoon baking soda	

PREP TIME: 15 MIN + 1–1½ HR FOR RISING 6–8 HR IF FROZEN

BAKE TIME: 45–50 MIN

1. In a large bowl, sprinkle yeast and 1 teaspoon sugar over the warm spring water. Stir until yeast dissolves completely. Let stand until foamy, about 5 minutes. Add salt, dry buttermilk, baking soda, remaining sugar, butter, and egg. Stir in 1½ cups flour. Using an electric mixer, beat at medium speed for 2 minutes, scraping bowl once or twice. Add onion and dill. Gradually beat in remaining flour. (Dough will still be soft and sticky.)

2. Place dough in a lightly greased 2-quart casserole. (At this point, you may wrap the casserole securely in plastic wrap, then aluminum foil, and freeze the batter for up to 2 weeks.)

3. When ready to bake, cover the casserole with a cloth. Let rise in a warm place until dough has doubled in bulk, 1 to 1½ hours (6 to 8 hours if frozen).

4. Place bread in a cold oven and turn on oven to 375°F. Bake until top is well browned and sounds hollow when tapped on the bottom, about 45 to 50 minutes. Let cool in casserole for 15 minutes. Turn out onto rack and cool. Serve at room temperature.

1 serving: 163 calories, 5 g protein, 3 g total fat (1.4 g saturated), 29 g carbohydrates, 224 mg sodium, 24 mg cholesterol, 1 g dietary fiber

DRIED CHERRY BREAD

About 75 percent of the nation's cherries are grown in the northern woods of Michigan. Thankfully, they are now available dried so we can enjoy them year round.

This delectable bread, sweetly spiced with cinnamon and scented with orange, is brimming with dried cherries. Try it thickly sliced for French Toast, sprinkled with confectioners' sugar.

½ cup sugar
½ teaspoon salt
1 package (¼ ounce) rapid-rise yeast
4 to 4½ cups unbleached all-purpose flour
1 cup canned evaporated whole milk
⅓ cup butter, cut into small pieces, at room temperature

1 large egg, slightly beaten
1 tablespoon ground cinnamon
½ cup dried cherries
⅓ cup chopped pecans
1 tablespoon grated orange rind

PREP TIME: 35 MIN + 40 MIN FOR RISING

BAKE TIME: 35–40 MIN

1. In a large bowl, combine sugar, salt, yeast, and 1 cup flour. In a saucepan, heat evaporated milk and butter over low heat until butter begins to melt and mixture reaches 120°F. Using medium speed of an electric mixer, gradually beat the milk mixture into the flour mixture. Continue beating for 2 minutes. Add egg and 1 cup of the flour; beat another 2 minutes. By hand, stir in another 2 cups of the flour.

2. **To knead with a dough hook,** beat on high speed until dough is springy and cleanly pulls away from the bowl, 5 to 7 minutes, adding up to ½ cup additional flour, 1 tablespoon at a time, as needed to keep dough from sticking. Turn dough out onto a lightly floured work surface. Cover and let rest for 15 minutes.

To knead by hand, turn dough out onto a lightly floured work surface and knead by hand until smooth and elastic, about 10 minutes, adding up to ½ cup additional flour, 1 tablespoon at a time, as needed to keep dough from sticking. Cover dough and let rest for 15 minutes.

3. Lightly grease a 9 x 5 x 3-inch loaf pan. Punch dough down and knead briefly on a lightly floured board to release the air. Form into a 9 x 12-inch rectangle. Sprinkle generously with cinnamon. Scatter cherries, pecans, and grated orange rind over the dough. Working from the 9-inch side, roll up jelly-roll-style into a cylinder, tucking ends under to seal. Place seam side down in prepared pan. Cover and let rise in a warm place until doubled in bulk, about 40 minutes.

4. Preheat oven to 350°F. Bake loaf until well browned, about 35 to 40 minutes. Let cool in pan for 5 minutes. Remove to rack to cool.

1 slice: 309 calories, 7 g protein, 10 g total fat (4.5 g saturated), 49 g carbohydrates, 170 mg sodium, 38 mg cholesterol, 2 g dietary fiber

FARMHOUSE SPINACH LOAF

MAKES 1 LOAF (12 SLICES)

If you have a kitchen garden, you probably grow spinach and basil. I can't think of a better use for their sprightly green leaves. When you clean the spinach and basil, you can shred any large spinach leaves and keep any very young stems intact. This savory bread makes splendid cheese sandwiches.

2 cups loosely packed fresh spinach leaves, tough stems removed, shredded

1 cup loosely packed fresh basil leaves, tough stems removed, shredded

1 small yellow onion, thinly sliced (½ cup)

1 tablespoon olive oil

1 large garlic clove, finely minced

1 package (¼ ounce) active dry yeast

1 tablespoon sugar

1¼ cups warm spring water, about 110°F

1 large egg, slightly beaten

½ teaspoon salt

¼ cup whole wheat flour

3 cups unbleached all-purpose flour

PREP TIME:
30 MIN +
1½ HR FOR
RISING

BAKE TIME:
40–45 MIN

1. Rinse spinach and basil leaves. Drain on paper towels and set aside to dry. Separate onion slices into separate rings. Set aside. In a small bowl, combine olive oil and garlic. Set aside.

2. In a large bowl, sprinkle yeast plus 1 teaspoon of the sugar over the warm spring water and stir until yeast dissolves completely. Let stand until foamy, about 5 minutes. Stir in the remaining 2 teaspoons sugar, the egg, salt, and the olive oil-garlic mixture. Stir the whole wheat flour and 2 cups of the all-purpose flour into the yeast mixture. Beat until well blended. Add another ½ cup of flour, ¼ cup at a time, beating after each addition.

3. Turn dough out onto a lightly floured work surface and knead by hand until smooth and elastic, about 10 minutes, adding up to ½ cup additional all-purpose flour, 1 tablespoon at a time, as needed to keep dough from sticking. Gradually knead in spinach, basil, and onion until evenly distributed.

4. Form dough into a ball and place in a lightly greased bowl, turning dough over once to coat top. Cover and let rise in a warm place until doubled in bulk, about 1 hour.

5. Punch down dough and knead briefly on a lightly floured board to release the air. Shape into a tight 7-inch round loaf and place on a greased baking sheet. Cover and let rise in a warm place until puffy, about 30 minutes.

6. Preheat oven to 350°F. Using a razor blade or sharp knife, make ¼-inch deep slashes on top of loaf in an X or cross-hatch design. Lightly dust top of loaf with flour. Bake, uncovered, until well browned, 40 to 45 minutes. Transfer bread to a rack to cool briefly. Serve warm.

1 slice: 150 calories, 5 g protein, 2 g total fat (0.4 g saturated), 28 g carbohydrates, 103 mg sodium, 18 mg cholesterol, 2 g dietary fiber

FRESH APPLE BRIOCHE

A brioche, a cross between a cake and a bread, is among the most popular sweet yeast breads. Apples and black pepper add flavor interest to this pretty topknot bread. Bake it in the 9-inch traditional fluted rim or in 3-inch individual brioche tins or giant muffins cups.

3 to 3½ cups unbleached all-purpose flour	2 large eggs, slightly beaten
1¼ teaspoons salt	2 medium Granny Smith or Paula Red apples,
2 teaspoons freshly cracked black peppercorns	peeled, cored, and diced (1¾ cups)
1 package (¼ ounce) active dry yeast	½ cup (1 stick) butter, at room temperature
1 tablespoon sugar	1 large egg yolk, beaten with 1 tablespoon
½ cup warm spring water, about 110°F	whole milk

PREP TIME: 25 MIN + 2 HR FOR RISING

BAKE TIME: 55–60 MIN (20–25 MIN FOR INDIVIDUAL BRIOCHES)

1. Combine 3 cups flour, salt, and pepper. Set aside.

2. In a large bowl, sprinkle yeast plus 1 teaspoon of the sugar over warm spring water and stir until yeast completely dissolves. Let stand until foamy, about 5 minutes. Stir in the remaining 2 teaspoons sugar, the whole eggs and the apples. Cut butter into small pieces and stir into yeast mixture. Gradually stir in the 3 cups seasoned flour.

3. Turn dough out onto a lightly floured work surface and knead by hand until dough is smooth and elastic, about 10 minutes, adding up to ½ cup additional flour, 1 tablespoon at a time, as needed to keep dough from sticking. Place dough in a lightly greased bowl, turning dough over once to coat top. Cover and let rise in a warm place until dough has doubled in bulk, about 1 hour. Punch down dough and knead briefly on a lightly floured work surface to release the air.

4. Pinch off a sixth of the dough and set aside. Shape the large portion into a smooth ball. Place dough smooth side up in a well buttered 9-inch fluted brioche pan or 2-quart round baking pan at least 8 inches deep, pressing dough down to fill the bottom of the pan.

5. Shape reserved piece of dough into a tear-drop or pear shape. With a sharp knife, poke a hole in the center of the large portion of dough through to the bottom of the pan. Place teardrop into this hole, inserting the point first.

6. Cover shaped brioche with a cloth and let rise in a warm place until doubled in bulk, about 1 hour.

7. Preheat oven to 375°F. Brush top of brioche with egg yolk mixture. Bake until well browned and a tester inserted in center comes out clean, about 55 to 60 minutes. (If brioche browns too quickly, cover loosely with aluminum foil.) Let cool in pan for 5 minutes. Remove and cool on a rack.

To make individual petite brioches: Cut dough into 12 equal pieces. Following the directions above, shape one at a time into individual brioches, keeping remaining dough refrigerated. Bake in well buttered 3-inch individual brioche tins or 3-inch muffin cups at 350°F until well browned and a tester inserted in center comes out clean, about 20 to 25 minutes. Cool as for large brioche.

1 serving or 1 small brioche: 228 calories, 5 g protein, 9 g total fat (5.3 g saturated), 31 g carbohydrates, 313 mg sodium, 74 mg cholesterol, 2 g dietary fiber

HARVEST SUNFLOWER BREAD

MAKES 2 LOAVES (12 SLICES EACH)

Sunflowers are the state flower of Kansas and grow rampant on my farms. Their seeds exude their flavorful oil and give this country loaf its dense texture. I buy jars of raw sunflower seeds at my natural food store. Store sunflower seeds in the refrigerator.

4½ to 5½ cups unbleached all-purpose flour	2 cups spring water
2 cups whole wheat flour	1 cup raw, hulled sunflower seeds
2 tablespoons sugar	1½ tablespoons mild vegetable oil, such as canola
2 packages (¼ ounce each) rapid-rise yeast	1 large egg beaten with 1 tablespoon water
6 tablespoons (¾ stick) butter	½ teaspoon coarse salt

**PREP TIME:
30 MIN + 45
MIN FOR RISING
BAKE TIME:
40–45MIN**

1. Set aside 1 cup all-purpose flour. In a large bowl, combine 4½ cups all-purpose flour, the whole wheat flour, sugar, and yeast.

2. In a small saucepan, heat butter and spring water until butter melts and mixture reaches 120°F. Stir into flour mixture along with the sunflower seeds until dough forms.

3. Turn dough out onto a lightly floured work surface and knead until dough is smooth and elastic, about 10 minutes, adding up to 1 cup of the reserved flour, 1 tablespoon at a time, as needed to keep dough from sticking. Cover dough and let rest for 10 minutes.

4. Divide dough in half and shape each portion into a round loaf, gently pulling top surface under until smooth. Place each loaf on a lightly greased baking sheet. Lightly brush with oil. Cover and let rise in a warm place until doubled in bulk, about 45 minutes.

5. Preheat oven to 375°F. Brush loaves with egg mixture. Using a razor blade or very sharp serrated knife, slash the top of each loaf in a simple, decorative pattern, cutting no more than ¼-inch deep. Sprinkle with coarse salt. Bake until golden brown and loaves sound hollow when tapped on the bottom, about 40 to 45 minutes. Cool on a rack. Serve warm.

1 slice: 205 calories, 6 g protein, 7 g total fat (2.3 g saturated), 30 g carbohydrates, 63 mg sodium, 17 mg cholesterol, 3 g dietary fiber

HEARTH LOAF

MAKES 1 LOAF (10 SLICES)

This rustic bread is similar in texture to the unleavened bread that was baked in the ashes of the campfires or cooking fireplaces when the Heartland was young. This version has two kinds of leavening to lighten the texture and cornmeal and fresh herbs for added flavor. Since it doesn't require any time for rising, it goes together like a quick bread.

1 package (¼ ounce) active dry yeast
1 teaspoon sugar
¼ cup warm spring water, about 110°F
1 cup warm whole milk, about 110°F
2¼ to 2½ cups unbleached all-purpose flour
½ cup stone ground cornmeal
1 tablespoon baking powder
½ teaspoon salt
3 tablespoons cold butter

1 tablespoon minced fresh thyme leaves
or 1 teaspoon dried thyme
1 tablespoon minced fresh tarragon
or 1 teaspoon dried tarragon
1 tablespoon minced fresh basil
or 1 teaspoon dried basil
1 large egg, slightly beaten with 1 tablespoon whole milk
½ teaspoon coarse salt

PREP TIME: 20 MIN
BAKE TIME: 40–45 MIN

1. Preheat oven to 375°F. Lightly grease a baking sheet.
2. In a small bowl, sprinkle yeast and sugar over warm spring water and stir until yeast dissolves completely. Let stand until foamy, about 5 minutes. Stir in milk; set aside.
3. In a large bowl, combine 2¼ cups of the flour, the cornmeal, baking powder, and salt. Using a pastry blender or two forks, cut in butter until mixture resembles coarse crumbs. Stir in herbs and yeast mixture. Mix until dough is evenly moistened.
4. Turn out onto a lightly floured work surface and knead briefly, about 5 minutes, adding up to ¼ cup additional flour, 1 tablespoon at a time, as needed to keep dough from sticking. Shape dough into a 6- to 7-inch round.
5. Brush loaf with egg mixture. With a razor blade or very sharp knife, make a deep X in the top of the loaf, cutting about ½-inch deep. Sprinkle with coarse salt. Bake for 40 to 45 minutes, until loaf is well browned and sounds hollow when tapped on the bottom. Transfer to a rack to cool. Serve warm.

1 slice: 198 calories, 6 g protein, 5 g total fat (2.9 g saturated), 32 g carbohydrates, 379 mg sodium, 34 mg cholesterol, 2 g dietary fiber

BLUE CHEESE SPREAD

MAKES 1 CUP

PREP TIME: 10 MIN • CHILL TIME: 4 TO 5 HR

    1 3-ounce package cream cheese, at room temperature
    3 ounces blue cheese such as Maytag, Stilton, or Saga, crumbled
    1 large garlic clove, mashed
    ½ teaspoon coarsely ground black pepper
    ½ cup (1 stick) butter, at room temperature

1. Using a food processor or by hand, combine all ingredients; process until thoroughly blended. Pack into a crock or shape into a log and wrap in plastic wrap or wax paper. Cover and refrigerate for 4 hours, or until firm. Serve within 4 days.
2. Bring to room temperature before serving.

1 tablespoon: 89 calories, 2 g protein, 9 g total fat (5.7 g saturated), trace carbohydrates, 149 mg sodium, 25 mg cholesterol, 0 dietary fiber

HERBED ROLLS

MAKES 12 ROLLS

These are spectacular rolls, filled with a pocket of savory herbs and onion. If you're using fresh herbs (fresh herbs make most everything taste better), pick them on a sunny morning after the dew is gone, clean the herbs, and pat dry with paper towels.

3 to 4 cups unbleached all-purpose flour
⅓ cup sugar
½ teaspoon salt
1 package (¼ ounce) rapid-rise yeast
1¼ cups spring water, about 120°F
3 large garlic cloves, minced
1 small onion, minced (½ cup)
2 tablespoons extra-virgin olive oil
1 tablespoon chopped fresh dill
 or 1 teaspoon dried dill

1 tablespoon chopped fresh tarragon
 or 1 teaspoon dried tarragon
1 tablespoon chopped fresh thyme
 or 1 teaspoon dried thyme
¼ teaspoon freshly ground pepper
1 large egg beaten with 2 teaspoons water
1 tablespoon sesame seeds

PREP TIME: 50 MIN + 30 MIN FOR RISING

BAKE TIME: 15–20 MIN

1. Set aside 1 cup of the flour. In a large bowl, combine 1 cup flour, the sugar, salt, and yeast. In a saucepan, heat water until it reaches 120°F. Using a whisk, beat the water into the flour mixture. Gradually add another 2 cups flour, ½ cup at a time, to form a soft dough.

2. Turn out dough onto a lightly floured work surface and knead until smooth and elastic, about 10 minutes, adding up to 1 cup of the reserved flour, 1 tablespoon at a time, as needed to keep dough from sticking. Cover dough and let rest for 20 minutes.

3. Meanwhile, in a heavy skillet over low heat, sauté the garlic and onion in olive oil until garlic is limp but not browned. Remove from heat; stir in the herbs and pepper. Set aside to cool.

4. Line a heavy baking sheet with parchment paper. Divide the dough into 12 equal pieces. If using fresh herbs, place ½ tablespoon (about 1 teaspoon if using dried herbs) of the herb mixture in the center of each piece.

5. Working on a lightly floured surface, shape each piece into a round roll, completely enclosing the herb mixture. Place the rolls 3 inches apart on prepared baking sheet. Cover and let rise in a warm place until rolls double in bulk, about 30 minutes.

6. Preheat oven to 350°F. Lightly brush tops of rolls with egg mixture. Sprinkle with sesame seeds. Bake until golden brown, about 15 to 20 minutes.

1 roll: 190 calories, 5 g protein, 4 g total fat (0.6 g saturated), 35 g carbohydrates, 96 mg sodium, 18 mg cholesterol, 2 g dietary fiber

HOME-STYLE WHITE BREAD

MAKES 3 LOAVES (12 SLICES EACH)

This is the kind of standard farmhouse bread that my mother made. The fine-texture bread is fabulous fresh from the oven. Since the recipe makes 3 loaves, there will be plenty for sandwiches, French toast, or my favorite — a wonderfully rich bread pudding for dessert.

4 cups whole milk	8 to 8 ½ cups unbleached all-purpose flour
3 packages (¼ ounce each) active dry yeast	3 tablespoons butter, at room temperature
1 tablespoon sugar	2 teaspoons salt

PREP TIME: 20 MIN + 1½ HR FOR RISING

BAKE TIME: 35–40 MIN

1. In a saucepan, scald milk by bringing it just to a boil and quickly removing it from the heat. Cool to 110°F. Let stand until foamy, about 5 minutes. Pour into a large bowl; sprinkle on yeast and sugar. Stir until yeast completely dissolves. Stir in 3 cups of the flour, the butter, and the salt.

2. **To knead with a dough hook,** gradually add another 5 cups of the all-purpose flour, ½ cup at a time, until mixture forms a stiff dough. Continue to beat on medium speed until dough is springy and cleanly pulls away from the bowl, 5 to 7 minutes, adding up to ½ cup additional flour, 1 tablespoon at a time, as needed to keep dough from sticking.

To knead by hand, beating with a wooden spoon, gradually add 5 cups of the all-purpose flour, ½ cup at a time, until mixture forms a stiff dough. Turn dough onto a lightly floured work surface and knead by hand until smooth and elastic, about 10 minutes, adding up to ½ cup additional flour, 1 tablespoon at a time, as needed to keep dough from sticking.

3. Place dough in a lightly greased bowl, turning dough over once to coat top. Cover and let rise in a warm place until doubled in bulk, about 45 minutes.

4. Lightly grease three 9 x 5 x 3-inch loaf pans. Punch down dough and knead briefly on a lightly floured work surface to release the air. Divide dough into 3 equal portions and shape each portion into a loaf. Place loaves in prepared pans, seam side down. Cover and place them in a warm place until dough rises ½ inch above the rim of the pan, about 45 minutes.

5. Meanwhile, preheat oven to 400°F. Using a razor blade or sharp serrated knife, slash the top of the loaf in a decorative pattern (see page 12). Bake until golden brown and loaves sound hollow when tapped on the bottom, about 35 to 40 minutes. Remove from oven and turn out immediately onto a wire rack to cool.

1 slice: 132 calories, 4 g protein, 2 g total fat (1.2 g saturated), 24 g carbohydrates, 142 mg sodium, 6 mg cholesterol, 1 g dietary fiber

MILLER'S FIVE-GRAIN BREAD

MAKES 2 LOAVES (12 SLICES EACH)

You can find the grains for this wholesome bread at a natural food store. Its distinctive flavor comes from millet, a tiny round grain that looks like mustard seeds. A native African grass, millet was introduced to the Midwest in the 1960's by students from India and Africa who came to Heartland state universities to study agriculture.

Excellent for sandwiches, this bread is also terrific cut into thick slices, grilled, and brushed with melted butter.

2 packages (¼ ounce each) active dry yeast
2 teaspoons sugar
3 cups warm spring water, about 110°F
1 cup whole millet
1 cup regular or quick-cooking rolled oats, uncooked
1 cup whole wheat flour

½ cup pearl barley
½ cup raw brown rice
¼ cup (½ stick) butter, melted
3 tablespoons honey
1½ teaspoons salt
5 to 6 cups unbleached all-purpose flour

1. In a large bowl, sprinkle yeast and sugar over warm spring water and stir until yeast completely dissolves. Let stand until foamy, about 5 minutes.

2. Meanwhile, in a food processor or blender, combine the millet, rolled oats, whole wheat flour, barley, and brown rice. Process until the mixture forms a fine textured whole grain flour.

3. **To knead with a dough hook,** using medium speed of mixer, blend butter, honey, and salt into the yeast mixture. Beat in the whole grain flour mixture. Gradually add 5 cups all-purpose flour, ½ cup at a time, until mixture forms a stiff dough. Continue to beat on medium speed until dough is springy and cleanly pulls away from the bowl, 5 to 7 minutes, adding up to 1 cup additional flour, 1 tablespoon at a time, as needed to keep dough from sticking.

**PREP TIME:
30 MIN +
1³/₄ HR FOR
RISING

BAKE TIME:
35–40 MIN**

   To knead by hand, using a wooden spoon, stir butter, honey, and salt into yeast mixture. Add the whole grain flour mixture and beat well. Gradually add 5 cups all-purpose flour, ½ cup at a time, until mixture forms a stiff dough. Turn dough onto a lightly floured work surface and knead by hand until smooth and elastic, about 10 minutes, adding up to 1 cup additional flour, 1 tablespoon at a time, as needed to keep dough from sticking.

4. Place dough in a lightly greased bowl, turning dough over once to coat top. Cover and let rise in a warm place until dough is doubled in bulk, about 1 hour.

5. Punch down dough and knead briefly on a lightly floured work surface to release the air. Divide dough in half and shape each portion into a round loaf. Place each loaf on a greased or parchment-lined baking sheet. Cover loosely with plastic wrap. Let stand in a warm place until doubled in bulk, about 45 minutes. Using a serrated knife, slash the tops of the loaves in a cross hatch or other decorative pattern, making each cut no more than ¼-inch deep (see page 12).

6. Meanwhile, preheat oven to 375°F. Bake until bread is golden brown and bread sounds hollow when tapped on the bottom, about 35 to 40 minutes. Cool on a rack.

1 slice: 201 calories, 5 g protein, 3 g total fat (1.3 g saturated), 39 g carbohydrates, 155 mg sodium, 5 mg cholesterol, 3 g dietary fiber

MOTHER'S SUNDAY BUTTERHORNS

MAKES 24 BUTTERHORNS

These melt-in-your-mouth dinner rolls were standard fare at my mother's Sunday dinner table. Just before baking, she'd brush the unbaked rolls with melted butter to give them a shiny, soft crust. I use an egg glaze, which results in a deeper color and a crispier crust.

If you like, you can add a handful of chopped fresh herbs to the dough before shaping (any combination of parsley, chervil, dill, chives, mint, thyme, or marjoram).

1 package (¼ ounce) active dry yeast	¾ cup whole milk
¼ cup warm spring water, about 110°F	3 to 3½ cups unbleached all-purpose flour
¼ cup sugar	EGG GLAZE
½ cup (1 stick) butter, at room temperature	2 large egg yolks beaten
1 teaspoon salt	with 1 tablespoon whole milk
2 large eggs, slightly beaten	¼ teaspoon sugar

**PREP TIME:
40 MIN + 1 ½
HR FOR RISING

BAKE TIME:
12–15 MIN**

1. Sprinkle yeast over warm spring water in a small bowl. Add 1 teaspoon of the sugar and stir until yeast dissolves completely. Let stand until foamy, about 5 minutes.

2. Meanwhile, in a large bowl, cream together remaining sugar, 6 tablespoons of the butter, and salt. Add eggs, one at a time, beating after each addition; whisk in the milk. Add yeast mixture to egg mixture. Gradually stir in 3 cups flour. Turn dough out onto a lightly floured work surface and knead in up to ½ cup additional flour, 1 tablespoon at a time, as needed to keep dough from sticking.

3. Place dough in a lightly greased bowl, turning dough over once to coat top. Cover and rise in a warm place until doubled in bulk, about 1 hour.

4. Punch down dough and knead briefly on a lightly floured work surface to release the air. Divide dough into 2 equal parts. Roll each part into a 9-inch circle. Melt remaining 2 tablespoons of butter and brush on dough. Cut each round into quarters, then each quarter into 3 equal triangles. Starting at wide end, roll up wedges toward the point to make butterhorns. Place 2 inches apart, points underneath, on a greased cookie sheet. Cover and let rise in a warm place until doubled in bulk, about 30 minutes.

5. Meanwhile, preheat oven to 375°F. In a small bowl, beat together egg glaze ingredients. Brush over rolls. Bake 12 to 15 minutes, until golden brown. Serve hot.

1 butterhorn: 121 calories, 3 g protein, 5 g total fat (2.9 g saturated), 16 g carbohydrates, 139 mg sodium, 47 mg cholesterol, 1 g dietary fiber

VARIATIONS: DINNER ROLLS

MAKES 18 ROLLS

The same dough can be shaped into Cloverleaf Rolls, Fantan Rolls or Bowknots. Shaped as such, a recipe makes 18 rolls.

CLOVERLEAF ROLLS

1, 2, and 3. Refer to steps 1, 2, and 3 for butterhorns.

4. Punch down dough and knead briefly on a lightly floured work surface to release the air. Divide dough into 2 equal parts. Using your hands, roll each part into a long cylinder about 18 inches long. Using a sharp knife, divide the cylinders in thirds and then cut each third into 3 equal pieces. Divide each of these 18 portions into three pieces for a total of 54 pieces, making all pieces about the same size.

5. Lightly grease 18 muffin cups. With your hands, lightly roll each piece of dough into a smooth ball. Place a cluster of 3 balls in each muffin cup. Omit egg glaze. Melt remaining 2 tablespoons butter and brush on rolls. Allow to rise until doubled in bulk, about 30 minutes. Bake in a preheated 375°F oven until golden, 20 to 25 minutes.

FANTAN ROLLS

1, 2, and 3. Refer to steps 1, 2, and 3 for butterhorns.

4. Punch down dough and knead briefly on a lightly floured work surface to release the air. Divide dough into two equal portions. Roll out one portion to form an 8 x 15-inch rectangle, ½-inch thick. Melt remaining 2 tablespoons butter and brush over dough. Cut into 5 lengthwise strips (15 inches x 1½ inches). Stack the five strips evenly and lightly press together. Using a very sharp knife, cut the strips into nine 1½-inch squares. Repeat with second portion of dough.

5. Lightly grease 18 standard muffin tins. Place each square in a muffin cup, cut side up. Brush with egg glaze and let rise until doubled in bulk, about 30 minutes. Bake in a preheated 375°F oven until golden, 20 to 25 minutes.

BOWKNOT ROLLS

1, 2, and 3. Refer to steps 1, 2, and 3 for butterhorns.

4. Punch down dough and briefly knead on a floured surface to release air. Divide dough into 2 equal parts. Using your hands, roll each part into a long cylinder about 18 inches long. Using a sharp knife, divide the cylinders in thirds and then cut each third into 3 equal pieces, forming a total of 18 pieces. Roll each piece into a smooth rope ½-inch in diameter and 9 to 10 inches long. Gently tie each length once as you would start to make a loose knot.

5. Place at least 2 inches apart on a greased baking sheet. Omit egg glaze. Melt remaining 2 tablespoons butter and brush on rolls. Let rise until doubled in bulk, about 30 minutes. Bake in a preheated 375°F oven until golden, 20 to 25 minutes.

1 roll: 162 calories, 4 g protein, 7 g total fat (3.8 g saturated), 21 g carbohydrates, 185 mg sodium, 63 mg cholesterol, 1 g dietary fiber

OLD-FASHIONED OATMEAL BREAD

MAKES 2 LOAVES (12 SLICES EACH)

A family favorite. Try it toasted for breakfast or with thinly sliced ripe tomatoes and Monterey Jack cheese melted on top for lunch. Raw oat bran is available at natural food stores and some larger supermarkets. You could substitute wheat bran for a slightly different taste.

2 packages (¼ ounce each) active dry yeast
2 teaspoons sugar
3 cups warm spring water, about 110°F
2 large eggs, slightly beaten
2 tablespoons honey
2 teaspoons salt
½ cup raw oat bran

2¼ cups quick-cook or regular rolled oats, uncooked
3 to 3½ cups unbleached all-purpose flour
2½ cups stone ground whole wheat flour
1 large egg white beaten with 1 tablespoon water

PREP TIME: 30 MIN + 1¾ HR FOR RISING
BAKE TIME: 30–35 MIN

1. In a large bowl, sprinkle yeast and sugar over water. Stir until yeast dissolves completely. Let stand until foamy, about 5 minutes. Stir in eggs, honey, and salt. Add the oat bran. Gradually stir in 2 cups of the oats.

2. Combine 3 cups of the all-purpose flour and the whole wheat flour. Add to the yeast mixture, ½ cup at a time, beating with a heavy spoon after each addition.

3. Turn out onto a lightly floured work surface and knead until dough is smooth and elastic, about 10 minutes, adding up to ½ cup additional flour mixture, 1 tablespoon at a time, as needed to keep dough from sticking. Place dough in a lightly greased bowl, turning dough over once to coat top. Cover and let rise in a warm place until doubled in bulk, about 1 hour.

4. Punch down dough and knead briefly on a lightly floured work surface to release the air. Divide dough in half and shape each portion into a loaf. Lightly grease two 9 x 5 x 3-inch loaf pans and place loaves seam side down in prepared pans. Cover and let rise until dough is ½ inch above the pan rim, about 45 minutes.

5. Preheat oven to 375°F. Brush the tops of both loaves with beaten egg white. Sprinkle on the remaining ¼ cup oats. Bake until the loaves are well browned, about 30 to 35 minutes. Cool on a rack.

1 slice: 153 calories, 6 g protein, 1 g total fat (0.3 g saturated), 30 g carbohydrates, 187 mg sodium, 18 mg cholesterol, 3 g dietary fiber

POPPY SEED BRAID

MAKES 2 LOAVES (12 SLICES EACH)

Poppy seeds have been decorating Heartland breads and cakes since the settlers first unloaded their covered wagons. Here the minute blue-black seeds from the poppy flower add crunch to this attractive bread. Terrific for morning toast, this bread also makes a distinctive grilled cheese sandwich.

2 packages (¼ ounce each) active dry yeast	2 large eggs, slightly beaten
2 tablespoons sugar	5½ to 6 cups unbleached all-purpose flour
1 cup warm spring water, about 110°F	¼ cup poppy seeds
1 cup warm whole milk, about 110°F	TOPPING
6 tablespoons butter, melted	1 large egg beaten with 1 tablespoon water
1½ teaspoons salt	2 tablespoons poppy seeds, for sprinkling

1. In a large bowl, sprinkle yeast and 2 teaspoons of the sugar over warm spring water. Stir until yeast dissolves completely. Let stand until foamy, about 5 minutes.

2. To knead with a dough hook, using medium speed of mixer, blend the remaining sugar, milk, butter, salt, and eggs into the yeast mixture. Beat in 1½ cups flour. Continue to beat on medium speed, gradually adding another 4 cups flour, ½ cup at a time. Add ¼ cup of the poppy seeds. Continue to beat until dough is springy and cleanly pulls away from the sides of the bowl, 5 to 7 minutes, adding up to ½ cup additional flour, 1 tablespoon at a time, as needed to keep dough from sticking.

PREP TIME: 30 MIN + 1¾ HR FOR RISING

BAKE TIME: 30–35 MIN

To knead by hand, mixing with a wooden spoon, combine the remaining sugar, milk, butter, salt, and eggs into the yeast mixture. Beat well. Stir in 3 cups flour. Gradually add another 2½ cups flour, ½ cup at a time. Stir in ¼ cup of the poppy seeds. Turn dough out onto a lightly floured work surface and knead by hand until dough is smooth and elastic, about 10 minutes, adding up to ½ cup additional flour, 1 tablespoon at a time, as needed to keep dough from sticking.

3. Place dough in a lightly greased bowl, turning dough over once to coat top. Cover and let rise in a warm place until dough is doubled in bulk, about 1 hour.

4. Punch down dough and knead briefly on a lightly floured work surface to release the air. Divide dough in half. Divide each half into 3 equal parts. On a lightly floured surface, roll each portion into a rope about 12 inches long. Place 3 of the ropes on a lightly greased baking sheet, crossing in the center. Braid out to each end, pinching ends together. Repeat

the procedure with the second portion, forming a second loaf. Lightly cover the loaves and let rise in a warm place until almost doubled in bulk, about 45 minutes. Brush the tops of both loaves with the beaten egg. Sprinkle the top of each loaf with 1 tablespoon poppy seeds.

5. Preheat oven to 350°F. (If bread browns too quickly, cover loosely with aluminum foil.) Bake until golden brown, about 30 to 35 minutes. Transfer to a rack to cool.

1 slice: 167 calories, 5 g protein, 5 g total fat (2.4 g saturated), 25 g carbohydrates, 177 mg sodium, 36 mg cholesterol, 1 g dietary fiber

PRAIRIE RYE BREAD

MAKES 2 LOAVES (12 SLICES EACH)

Unlike breads of earlier times when raisins were scarce and used sparingly, this light rye loaf is full of plump raisins. An earthy, strongly flavored grain similar to wheat, rye thrives on the cold winters of the Heartland, and was one of the first grains planted by settlers immigrating from eastern Europe.

This bread is wonderful for morning French Toast or nibbling any time of the day. The sponge needs 6 hours, so plan ahead.

SPONGE

1½ cups coarsely ground light rye flour
2 packages (¼ ounce each) active dry yeast
2½ cups warm spring water, about 110°F

DOUGH

2 cups golden raisins
Boiling water
1½ cups coarsely ground light rye flour

1 tablespoon caraway seeds
3 tablespoons butter, melted and cooled
 to room temperature
1 teaspoon salt
4½ to 5 cups unbleached all-purpose flour,
 plus 2 teaspoons for dusting loaves
1 large egg, beaten with 1 tablespoon water
 Additional caraway seeds, optional

**PREP TIME:
50 MIN + 6 HR
RESTING TIME FOR
SPONGE AND 1¾ HR
FOR RISING**

**BAKE TIME:
40–45 MIN**

1. Six hours ahead, prepare the sponge by combining the 1½ cups light rye flour, the yeast, and water in a large bowl. Stir well. Cover with plastic wrap and let stand at room temperature for 6 hours.

2. When the sponge is ready, place raisins in a small bowl. Add boiling water to cover. Let stand until raisins are plump, about 10 minutes. Drain well. Set aside.

3. Meanwhile, stir another 1½ cups light rye flour into the prepared sponge. Add caraway seeds, butter, and salt, stirring to blend well. Gradually stir in 4½ cups all-purpose flour. Turn dough out onto a lightly floured work surface and knead by hand for 5 minutes, adding up to ½ cup additional flour, 1 tablespoon at a time, as needed to keep dough from sticking.

4. Pat dough to a large rectangle. Spread raisins over dough. Fold dough, enclosing raisins, completely. Continue kneading until smooth and elastic, about 5 minutes, adding more flour if dough is sticky. Place dough in a lightly greased bowl, turning dough over once to coat top. Cover and let rise in a warm place until doubled in bulk, about 1 hour.

5. Punch down dough and knead briefly on a lightly floured work surface to release the air. Divide dough in half. Shape each half into a 7-inch round loaf and place smooth side up on lightly oiled baking sheets. Dust the top of each loaf with 1 teaspoon flour and cover lightly with plastic wrap. Let rise in a warm place until doubled in bulk, about 45 minutes.

6. Preheat oven to 350°F. Using a razor blade or sharp knife, make ¼-inch deep slashes on top of each loaf in an X or cross-hatch design. Brush the loaves with beaten egg. Sprinkle with additional caraway seeds if desired. Bake until deep brown and bread sounds hollow when tapped on bottom, about 40 to 45 minutes. Cool on a rack.

1 slice: 198 calories, 5 g protein, 2 g total fat (1.0 g saturated), 41 g carbohydrates, 109 mg sodium, 13 mg cholesterol, 3 g dietary fiber

PUFFY POTATO ROLLS

MAKES 12 ROLLS

Potato bread has always been a favorite of mine and most everyone else from the Midwest. So are these little puffy rolls. Serve them with an herb butter (page 64).

Yeast thrives on potato starch and produces a fluffy texture that is a characteristic of potato bread.

3 cups unbleached all-purpose flour
1 package (¼ ounce) rapid-rise yeast
1 tablespoon sugar
1 teaspoon salt
1 medium russet potato, peeled and shredded (1 cup)

¾ cup whole milk
3 tablespoons butter, at room temperature
¼ teaspoon liquid hot pepper sauce
1 large egg, slightly beaten

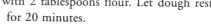

PREP TIME:
35 MIN + 40 MIN
FOR RISING
BAKE TIME:
20–25 MIN

1. In the workbowl of a food processor, combine 2¾ cups of the flour, yeast, sugar, salt, and potato.

2. In a small saucepan, heat milk, 2 tablespoons of the butter, and the liquid hot pepper sauce until butter melts and milk reaches 120°F. With food processor running, quickly pour in milk mixture through the feed tube. Add the egg and process until dough forms a ball. Continue to process until dough is elastic, about 1 minute. (Dough will be quite soft.)

3. Turn dough out onto a lightly floured work surface and sprinkle with 2 tablespoons flour. Let dough rest for 20 minutes.

4. Sprinkle dough with the remaining 2 tablespoons flour and lightly knead for about 1 minute. (Dough will be soft.) Roll dough into a 12-inch log. Cut into 12 equal pieces.

5. Grease a 9-inch round cake pan. With fingertips, shape each piece into a ball, tucking the edges underneath to make a smooth top. Arrange in prepared pan. Cover with a towel. Let rise in a warm place until doubled in bulk, about 40 minutes.

6. Preheat oven to 350°F. Bake buns until golden brown, about 20 to 25 minutes. Brush with the remaining 1 tablespoon butter. Serve warm.

1 roll: 168 calories, 5 g protein, 4 g total fat (2.3 g saturated), 28 g carbohydrates, 221 mg sodium, 28 mg cholesterol, 1 g dietary fiber

RUSTIC BLACK PEPPER AND WALNUT BREAD

MAKES 2 LOAVES (8 SLICES EACH)

Black walnuts are plentiful throughout much of middle America and add a unique flavor to this savory bread. When I was growing up, we'd spend the better part of a fall weekend gathering, cracking, and shelling a supply of black walnuts.

If you can't get black walnuts, substitute the more common English variety. This very dense bread requires little kneading so it goes together quickly. The finished loaf resembles the flat, irregular loaves originally baked directly on the hearth. If you'd prefer a higher loaf and lighter texture, allow the unbaked loaf to rise in a warm place for 45 minutes before baking.

1½ cups warm spring water, about 110°F	3 cups plus 2 tablespoons unbleached all-purpose flour
1 package (¼ ounce) active dry yeast	¾ cup coarsely chopped black walnuts
1 tablespoon sugar	1 tablespoon freshly cracked black peppercorns
1½ teaspoons salt	

1. In a large bowl, sprinkle yeast and 1 teaspoon of the sugar over warm spring water. Stir until yeast dissolves completely. Let stand until foamy, about 5 minutes. Stir in the remaining 2 teaspoons sugar and the salt. Add 3 cups of the flour, 1 cup at a time, mixing to form a soft dough.

2. Place dough in a lightly greased bowl, turning dough over once to coat top. Let the dough rise in a warm place until doubled in bulk, about 40 minutes.

3. Punch down dough and knead briefly on a lightly floured board to release the air. Pat dough into a large, thick rectangle. Toss remaining 2 tablespoons flour with the walnuts and peppercorns. Evenly sprinkle onto the top of the dough and with your fingers press the mixture into the dough. Fold over and knead briefly to evenly distribute, about 3 minutes. Divide dough in half and form into 2 rounded loaves of equal size. With your fingers, press dough down around the edges of each loaf, forming what resembles the rim of a hat. If you prefer a lighter loaf, cover the loaves and let rise in a warm place for 45 minutes.

PREP TIME: 20 MIN + 40 MIN FOR RISING

BAKE TIME: 20-25 MIN

4. Preheat oven to 450°F. Place the oven rack on the next to the top rack position. Place a double layer of heavy duty aluminum foil on the rack. Lay formed loaves directly on the foil. Bake for 12 to 15 minutes, until browned. Flip loaves over and bake another 8 to 10 minutes. Serve warm.

1 slice: 129 calories, 4 g protein, 4 g total fat (0.3 g saturated), 20 g carbohydrates, 201 mg sodium, 0 cholesterol, 1 g dietary fiber

WISCONSIN CHEESE BREAD

MAKES 1 LOAF (12 SLICES)

When I think of the dairy state, its wonderful sharp Cheddar immediately comes to mind. This bread puts it to memorable use.

Toast a slice and top with a poached egg for a breakfast or a simple supper.

3 to 3 ½ cups unbleached all-purpose flour
1 package (¼ ounce) rapid-rise yeast
1 tablespoon sugar
1 teaspoon salt
1 teaspoon dried red pepper flakes
¾ cup canned evaporated whole milk

¼ cup spring water
1½ tablespoons mild vegetable oil, such as canola
¼ cup (½ stick) butter, melted
2 cups firmly packed grated sharp Wisconsin Cheddar cheese (8 ounces)

**PREP TIME:
50 MIN + 45 MIN
FOR RISING
BAKE TIME:
15–20 MIN**

1. In a large bowl, mix together 2½ cups flour, yeast, sugar, salt, and red pepper flakes.

2. In a small saucepan, combine evaporated milk, water, and oil. Heat until mixture reaches 120°F. Stir into the flour mixture.

3. Turn dough out onto a lightly floured work surface and knead until smooth and elastic, about 10 minutes, adding up to 1 cup additional flour, 1 tablespoon at a time, as needed to keep dough from sticking. Knead 1 cup of the cheese into the dough. Cover dough and let rest for 15 minutes.

4. Lightly oil an 8 x 5 x 3-inch loaf pan. Divide dough in half and cut each half into 8 equal pieces. Shape each piece into a ball, coating with some of the melted butter. Arrange 8 balls in a single layer in the prepared loaf pan. Sprinkle with ½ cup of the remaining cheese. Place remaining 8 balls in a single layer on top of the cheese. Sprinkle with remaining cheese. Cover and let rise in a warm place until doubled in bulk, about 45 minutes.

5. Preheat oven to 400°F. Bake loaf until well browned, about 15 to 20 minutes, covering loosely with a sheet of aluminum foil if cheese browns too quickly. Turn out onto a rack and cool completely before slicing.

1 slice: 275 calories, 10 g protein, 13 g total fat (7.3 g saturated), 29 g carbohydrates, 351 mg sodium, 35 mg cholesterol, 1 g dietary fiber

BREAD MACHINE BREADS

BREAD MACHINES ARE EASY TO USE, but they do require that you measure ingredients precisely and put them in the bread pan in the order suggested in your owner's manual. For recipe consistency, I have listed water first and yeast last, followed by any ingredients to be added towards the end of, or after, the first knead. And for best results, bring all ingredients to room temperature before mixing up these bread machine recipes.

Baking times vary from machine to machine, whether you are using the regular, rapid, or delayed bake cycle. For best results, use these recipes with your bread machine manufacturer's instructions.

As in my other bread recipes, I call for spring water. In bread machines, it's particularly important that the action of the yeast not be sabotaged by heavily chlorinated water, since yeast is a (beneficial) fungus and chlorine is a chemical for killing fungus. If you have well water or you know that your water is not heavily chlorinated, you can use water from the tap with good results.

Bread machines can't compensate for variations in humidity and ingredients. That's why a recipe that's successful in the dry heat of summer may not work well on a rainy day in the spring or fall. Also, flours milled from wheat grown in different states vary greatly; therefore, your bread baking success may also vary from state to state, even when using the same recipe and the same bread machine.

It's important to watch the dough during the first few minutes of the first mix-knead cycle. The dough should form a soft ball and cleanly pull away from the sides of the bread pan. If the weather is quite humid and the dough is too wet, you can add an additional 1 to 2 tablespoons of flour. Conversely, if the dough is dry and crumbly, add water, a tablespoon at a time, until the dough reaches the right consistency. This proper balance between flour and liquid is essential to a good loaf. When making conventional yeast breads, you accomplish the same result by adding additional flour while you are kneading to keep the dough from sticking. If you wish to add additional ingredients, such as chopped nuts, poppy seeds, oats to decorate the top of the loaf prior to baking, consult your manufacturer's manual to determine how far into the cycle the baking begins. After that, it's best to not open the lid again until the baking is completed.

When using a bread making machine at altitudes above 3,000 feet you may experience your bread crashing while baking. Try reducing the yeast by ¼ teaspoon at a time to slow the rising. Also experiment with reducing the water by no more than 2 tablespoons.

Do not use the delayed bake cycle if a recipe calls for eggs or fresh milk products since these ingredients are extremely perishable.

NUTRITIONAL INFORMATION

FOR EACH RECIPE A NUTRITIONAL ANALYSIS IS PROVIDED, stating calorie count; grams of protein, total fat and saturated fat, carbohydrates, and dietary fiber; and milligrams of sodium and cholesterol. Calculated by software provided by "The Food Processor," Version 6.02, by ESHA Research, the analysis applies to a single serving, based on the number of servings given for each recipe.

For breads baked in a bread baking machine, the nutritional information is based on 8 servings for a 1-pound loaf and 12 servings for a 1½-pound loaf as baked on a regular bake cycle. If you choose to bake a recipe on a rapid bake cycle, the loaf will be smaller and more compact. Therefore, you will need to slice the bread in the same number of pieces, yet thinner slices, in order to comply with the nutritional data as provided.

BEST EVER WHITE BREAD

MAKES ONE 1-POUND LOAF (8 SLICES) OR 1 1/2-POUND LOAF (12 SLICES)

This is a fabulous white bread, perfect for sandwiches, morning toast, or homemade croutons.

Since the recipe calls for dry buttermilk (look for it in the baking goods aisle or near the dry nonfat milk at your supermarket), it needs a smidgeon of baking soda. Dry buttermilk is also available by mail-order (see Sources, page 142), but if you don't have it, you can use dry nonfat milk (omitting the baking soda) which will produce a bread with a finer texture. You could also replace the water with fresh cultured low-fat (1.5%) buttermilk as long as you aren't using the delayed bake cycle.

1-POUND LOAF	1 ½-POUND LOAF
1 cup spring water (75 to 80°F)	1 cup plus 2 tablespoons spring water (75 to 80°F)
2 cups white bread flour	3 cups white bread flour
3 tablespoons dry buttermilk	¼ cup dry buttermilk
¼ teaspoon baking soda	½ teaspoon baking soda
2 teaspoons sugar	1 tablespoon sugar
1 teaspoon salt	1½ teaspoons salt
1 tablespoon butter, at room temperature	2 tablespoons butter, at room temperature
1 teaspoon rapid-rise yeast or 2 teaspoons active dry yeast	2 teaspoons rapid-rise yeast or 1 tablespoon active dry yeast

RECIPE NOT APPROPRIATE FOR DELAYED BAKE CYCLE IF USING FRESH BUTTERMILK

1. Put ingredients in the bread pan and assemble the bread machine according to manufacturer's instructions.
2. Select regular, rapid, or delayed bake cycle and medium crust setting.
3. Bake and cool as directed.

1 slice: 131 calories, 5 g protein, 2 g total fat (1.2 g saturated), 23 g carbohydrates, 338 mg sodium, 6 mg cholesterol, 1 g dietary fiber

BLUE RIBBON RYE BREAD

MAKES ONE 1-POUND LOAF (8 SLICES) OR 1 1/2-POUND LOAF (12 SLICES)

When the harvest is in, good cooks across the Midwest vie for blue-ribbon glory. The flavor of this bread would make it a winner — a light rye bread, orange scented with fennel seeds rather than the traditional caraway. Try this with cream cheese and thinly sliced smoked salmon for Sunday brunch.

1-POUND LOAF

⅓ cup spring water (75 to 80°F)
2 tablespoons fresh orange juice
1½ cups white bread flour
½ cup rye flour
1½ tablespoons dry nonfat milk
2 teaspoons sugar
1½ tablespoons butter, at room temperature
1 teaspoon rapid-rise yeast
  or 2 teaspoons active dry yeast
½ teaspoon dried orange peel
1 teaspoon fennel seeds

1½-POUND LOAF

1 cup spring water (75 to 80°F)
¼ cup fresh orange juice
2¼ cups white bread flour
¾ cup rye flour
2 tablespoons dry nonfat milk
1 tablespoon sugar
2 tablespoons butter, at room temperature
2 teaspoons rapid-rise yeast
  or 1 tablespoon active dry yeast
¾ teaspoon dried orange peel
1½ teaspoons fennel seeds

RECIPE WORKS BEST ON REGULAR BAKE CYCLE

1. Put all ingredients except dried orange peel and fennel seeds in the bread pan and assemble the bread machine according to manufacturer's instructions.

2. Select regular, rapid, or delayed bake cycle and light crust setting.

3. After the first beep or towards the end of the first knead, add the dried orange peel and fennel seeds, following your bread machine's instructions for raisin bread. Bake and cool as directed.

1 slice: 129 calories, 4 g protein, 3 g total fat (1.5 g saturated), 22 g carbohydrates, 29 mg sodium, 6 mg cholesterol, 2 g dietary fiber

BUTTERMILK BREAD WITH POPPY SEEDS

MAKES ONE 1-POUND LOAF (8 SLICES) OR 1 1/2-POUND LOAF (12 SLICES)

This delicious bread gets its crunchy texture from poppy seeds and cracked wheat, a grain milled by breaking whole wheat kernels with a coarse grindstone. If you can't find dry buttermilk in your supermarket (see Sources, page 142 for mail-order), you can replace the water with fresh cultured low-fat (1.5%) buttermilk as long as you are not using the delayed bake cycle. Depending on the humidity, you may also need to add 1 to 2 table-spoons additional flour.

Try this bread Midwest-style with meatloaf, just-picked tomatoes, and thinly sliced gherkins for a sublime sandwich, or serve it toasted with Quick Peach Marmalade (page 126) for a special breakfast treat.

1-POUND LOAF	1 ½-POUND LOAF
¾ cup plus 2 tablespoons spring water (75 to 80°F)	1⅓ cups spring water (75 to 80°F)
2 cups white bread flour	3 cups white bread flour
¼ cup cracked wheat	⅓ cup cracked wheat
3 tablespoons dry buttermilk	⅓ cup dry buttermilk
¼ teaspoon baking soda	½ teaspoon baking soda
1½ tablespoons sugar	2 tablespoons sugar
1 teaspoon salt	1½ teaspoons salt
1½ tablespoons butter, at room temperature	2 tablespoons butter, at room temperature
1½ teaspoons rapid-rise yeast or 2 teaspoons active dry yeast	2 teaspoons rapid-rise yeast or 1 tablespoon active dry yeast
2 teaspoons poppy seeds	1 tablespoon poppy seeds

RECIPE NOT APPROPRIATE FOR DELAYED BAKE CYCLE IF USING FRESH BUTTERMILK

1. Put all ingredients except poppy seeds in the bread pan and assemble the bread machine according to manufacturer's instructions.

2. Select regular, rapid, or delayed bake cycle and light crust setting.

3. After the first beep or towards the end of the first knead, add the poppy seeds, following your bread machine's instructions for raisin bread. Bake and cool as directed.

1 slice: 163 calories, 6 g protein, 4 g total fat (1.7 g saturated), 28 g carbohydrates, 345 mg sodium, 8 mg cholesterol, 2 g dietary fiber

CINNAMON CURRANT TOASTING LOAF

MAKES ONE 1-POUND (8 SLICES) OR 1 1/2-POUND LOAF (12 SLICES)

Both red and black currants grew wild on my grandfather's Kansas farm. Related to the gooseberry, they were good for out-of-hand eating. This delicious loaf calls for dried black currants, actually seedless, dried Zante grapes, which are readily available at the store. A good choice for breakfast. Its enticing aroma will lure sleepy appetites out of bed. If dry buttermilk is not available, you could replace the water with fresh cultured low-fat (1.5%) buttermilk as long as you are not using the delayed bake cycle.

1-POUND LOAF

¾ cup spring water (75 to 80°F)
2 cups white bread flour
2 tablespoons dry buttermilk
¼ teaspoon baking soda
1½ tablespoons sugar
1 teaspoon salt
1½ tablespoons butter, at room temperature
¾ teaspoon ground cinnamon
1½ teaspoons rapid-rise yeast
or 2 teaspoons active dry yeast
⅓ cup dried currants

1½-POUND LOAF

1 cup plus 2 tablespoons spring water
(75 to 80°F)
3 cups white bread flour
3 tablespoons dry buttermilk
½ teaspoon baking soda
2 tablespoons sugar
1½ teaspoons salt
2 tablespoons butter, at room temperature
1¼ teaspoons ground cinnamon
2 teaspoons rapid-rise yeast
or 1 tablespoon active dry yeast
½ cup dried currants

RECIPE NOT APPROPRIATE FOR DELAYED BAKE CYCLE IF USING FRESH BUTTERMILK

1. Put all ingredients except currants in the bread pan and assemble the bread machine according to manufacturer's instructions.
2. Select regular, rapid, or delayed bake cycle and light crust setting.
3. After the first beep or towards the end of the first knead, add the currants, following your bread machine's instructions for raisin bread. Bake and cool as directed.

1 slice: 156 calories, 5 g protein, 3 g total fat (1.6 g saturated), 28 g carbohydrates, 341 mg sodium, 7 mg cholesterol, 1 g dietary fiber

COUNTRY ROLLS

MAKES 8 ROLLS (1-POUND DOUGH) OR 12 ROLLS (1 1/2-POUND DOUGH)

Sunday dinner in the Heartland usually features freshly baked rolls. An electric bread making machine makes the preparation easy. Your machine mixes and kneads the dough — all you have to do is shape and bake them. The rolls are not brushed with butter prior to or after baking so they have a wonderful, crisp crust. Since this recipe calls for a fresh egg, do not use the delayed bake cycle.

Serve them warm from the oven with sweet butter or fresh goat cheese.

1-POUND DOUGH (8 ROLLS)

½ cup spring water (75 to 80°F)
1 large egg
2 cups white bread flour
1 tablespoon nonfat dry milk
1 tablespoon sugar
1 teaspoon salt
2 tablespoons olive oil
1 teaspoon rapid-rise yeast
   or 2 teaspoons active dry yeast
1 tablespoon white cornmeal
1 tablespoon coarse salt, for sprinkling

1 ½-POUND DOUGH (12 ROLLS)

¾ cup plus 2 tablespoons spring water (75 to 80°F)
1 large egg
3 cups white bread flour
1½ tablespoons nonfat dry milk
1½ tablespoons sugar
1½ teaspoons salt
3 tablespoons olive oil
2 teaspoons rapid-rise yeast
   or 1 tablespoon active dry yeast
2 tablespoons white cornmeal
1½ tablespoon coarse salt, for sprinkling

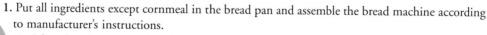

RECIPE NOT APPROPRIATE FOR DELAYED BAKE CYCLE

1. Put all ingredients except cornmeal in the bread pan and assemble the bread machine according to manufacturer's instructions.

2. Select dough or manual cycle.

3. When the machine beeps or after the manual cycle is completed, remove the dough from the machine and turn out onto a lightly floured work surface. Punch dough down and divide dough into 4 equal portions. Divide each quarter into 2 equal portions (for 1-pound dough) or 3 equal portions (for 1½-pound dough).

4. Form each portion into a round or oval and dust lightly all over with flour. Place rolls about 2 inches apart on a greased or parchment-lined baking sheet which has been dusted with the cornmeal. With a serrated knife, quickly make a slash about ¼-inch deep down the middle of each roll. Cover loosely with plastic wrap and let rest for 15 minutes. Sprinkle rolls lightly with coarse salt.

5. Meanwhile, preheat oven to 450°F. Place rolls in oven and immediately reduce the oven heat to 400°F. Bake until rolls are golden brown, 12 to 15 minutes. Serve hot from the oven.

1 roll: 166 calories, 5 g protein, 5 g total fat (0.8 g saturated), 26 g carbohydrates, 880 mg sodium, 27 mg cholesterol, 1 g dietary fiber

EGG CHEESE BREAD

MAKES ONE 1-POUND (8 SLICES) OR 1 1/2-POUND LOAF (12 SLICES)

This bread, richly flavored with eggs and Swiss cheese, would be delicious served with a hearty soup or main-dish salad. It's best served warm.

Feel free to substitute other cheeses for the Swiss: a sharp Cheddar, mild Monterey Jack, or another semifirm cheese of your liking.

1-POUND LOAF	1 ½-POUND LOAF
½ cup spring water (75 to 80°F)	¾ cup spring water (75 to 80°F)
2 cups white bread flour	3 cups white bread flour
1 tablespoon sugar	2 tablespoons sugar
1 teaspoon salt	1½ teaspoons salt
3 tablespoons butter, at room temperature	5 tablespoons butter, at room temperature
3 large egg yolks	4 large egg yolks
½ cup grated Swiss cheese	¾ cup grated Swiss cheese
1 teaspoon rapid-rise yeast or 2 teaspoons active dry yeast	2 teaspoons rapid-rise yeast or 1 tablespoon active dry yeast

RECIPE NOT APPROPRIATE FOR DELAYED BAKE CYCLE

1. Put all ingredients except 1 tablespoon of the cheese in the bread pan and assemble the bread machine according to manufacturer's instructions.
2. Select regular or rapid bake cycle and light crust setting.
3. After the first beep or towards the end of the first knead, sprinkle the reserved cheese on top of the bread. Bake and cool as directed.

1 slice: 195 calories, 7 g protein, 9 g total fat (4.7 g saturated), 22 g carbohydrates, 333 mg sodium, 98 mg cholesterol, 1 g dietary fiber

ENGLISH MUFFIN LOAF

MAKES ONE 1-POUND (8 SLICES)
OR 1 1/2-POUND LOAF (12 SLICES)

This lovely bread tastes something like English muffins and is wonderful toasted and topped with Cherry Jam (page 125) for breakfast or a perfect bedtime snack. The instant mashed potatoes give it a mealy texture that's characteristic of English muffins.

1-POUND LOAF	1½-POUND LOAF
¾ cup spring water (75 to 80°F)	1 cup spring water (75 to 80°F)
1¾ cups white bread flour	2½ cups white bread flour
¼ cup stone-ground whole wheat flour	⅓ cup stone-ground whole wheat flour
1 tablespoon nonfat dry milk	1½ tablespoons nonfat dry milk
2 teaspoons sugar	1 tablespoon sugar
1 teaspoon salt	1½ teaspoons salt
1 tablespoon instant mashed potatoes	2 tablespoons instant mashed potatoes
1 tablespoon butter, at room temperature	2 tablespoons butter, at room temperature
1¼ teaspoons rapid-rise yeast	2 teaspoons rapid-rise yeast
or 2 teaspoons active dry yeast	or 1 tablespoon active dry yeast

RECIPE WORKS BEST ON REGULAR OR DELAYED BAKE CYCLE

1. Put ingredients in the bread pan and assemble the bread machine according to manufacturer's instructions.

2. Select regular, rapid, or delayed bake cycle and light crust setting.

3. Bake and cool as directed.

1 slice: 128 calories, 4 g protein, 2 g total fat (1.1 g saturated), 23 g carbohydrates, 288 mg sodium, 4 mg cholesterol, 1 g dietary fiber

FRESH HERB LOAF

MAKES ONE 1-POUND LOAF (8 SLICES)
OR 1 1/2-POUND LOAF (12 SLICES)

Herbs have played a significant role in Midwestern food since the early settlers planted herb gardens. Today, even the plainest cooks rely on fresh herbs. You can vary the fresh herbs in this fragrant loaf according to what you grow in your garden or can buy at the store. Dill, tarragon, chives, and chervil would also make a delightful combination, used in the same amounts as the herbs in the recipe below.

A perfect loaf for avocado and tomato sandwiches, it also makes superb croutons for soups and salads or bread crumbs to top your favorite casserole.

1-POUND LOAF	1½-POUND LOAF
¾ cup spring water (75 to 80°F)	1¼ cups spring water (75 to 80°F)
2 cups white bread flour	3 cups white bread flour
1 tablespoon nonfat dry milk	1½ tablespoons nonfat dry milk
1 tablespoon sugar	1½ tablespoons sugar
½ teaspoon salt	1 teaspoon salt
1½ tablespoons butter, at room temperature	2 tablespoons butter, at room temperature
2 large egg yolks	3 large egg yolks
1 teaspoon rapid-rise yeast or 2 teaspoons active dry yeast	2 teaspoons rapid-rise yeast or 1 tablespoon active dry yeast
2 teaspoons minced fresh basil	1 tablespoon minced fresh basil
2 teaspoons minced fresh parsley	1 tablespoon minced fresh parsley
2 teaspoons minced fresh rosemary	1 tablespoon minced fresh rosemary
2 teaspoons minced fresh savory	1 tablespoon minced fresh savory
2 large garlic cloves, minced	3 large garlic cloves, minced

RECIPE NOT APPROPRIATE FOR DELAYED BAKE CYCLE

1. Put all ingredients except herbs and garlic in the bread pan and assemble the bread machine according to manufacturer's instructions.
2. Select regular or rapid bake cycle and light crust setting.
3. After the first beep or towards the end of the first knead, add the minced herbs and garlic, following your bread machine's instructions for raisin bread. Bake and cool as directed.

1 slice: 147 calories, 5 g protein, 4 g total fat (1.9 g saturated), 23 g carbohydrates, 163 mg sodium, 59 mg cholesterol, 1 g dietary fiber

GARLIC PARMESAN BREAD

MAKES ONE 1-POUND (8 SLICES)
OR 1 1/2-POUND LOAF (12 SLICES)

I love the smell of this bread as it's baking. Love it or hate it, garlic is the most widely used herb in the world and its influence is quite evident in Heartland cooking.

Here garlic adds warmth and excitement to a crusty home-baked bread. Slice it thick to spread with Brie and top with slivers of oil-packed sun-dried tomatoes as an appetizer or snack.

1-POUND LOAF

- ¾ cup spring water (75 to 80°F)
- 2 cups white bread flour
- 3 tablespoons grated Parmesan cheese
- ½ teaspoon salt
- 1 tablespoon nonfat dry milk
- 1 tablespoon olive oil
- 2 teaspoons sugar
- 2 teaspoons dried basil
- 1 teaspoon rapid-rise yeast
  or 2 teaspoons active dry yeast
- 4 large garlic cloves, finely slivered

1½-POUND LOAF

- 1 cup plus 2 tablespoons spring water (75 to 80°F)
- 3 cups white bread flour
- ⅓ cup grated Parmesan cheese
- 1 teaspoon salt
- 2 tablespoons nonfat dry milk
- 1½ tablespoons olive oil
- 1 tablespoon sugar
- 1 tablespoon dried basil
- 2 teaspoons rapid-rise yeast
  or 1 tablespoon active dry yeast
- 6 large garlic cloves, finely slivered

RECIPE WORKS BEST ON REGULAR BAKE CYCLE

1. Put all ingredients except the slivered garlic in the bread pan and assemble the bread machine according to manufacturer's instructions.

2. Select regular or rapid, or delayed bake cycle and light crust setting.

3. After the first beep or towards the end of the first knead, add the slivered garlic, following your bread machine's instructions for raisin bread. Bake and cool as directed.

1 slice: 138 calories, 5 g protein, 3 g total fat (0.9 g saturated), 23 g carbohydrates, 183 mg sodium, 2 mg cholesterol, 1 g dietary fiber

FOCACCIA BREAD

Flat breads are becoming quite popular in the Heartland and this hearty loaf makes a terrific focaccia-type bread if the dough or manual cycle is used and the bread is baked in the oven.

To make focaccia, remove the dough from the bread pan when the machine beeps or after the dough or manual cycle is completed. (Do not add slivered garlic to dough.) Pat the dough into two or three roughly round shapes about ½-inch thick. Place each loaf on a pizza stone or baking sheet which has been lightly greased or lined with parchment paper. Brush the top with a little olive oil, sprinkle with the slivered garlic, and bake in a preheated 450°F oven, reducing to 400°F when the bread goes into the oven, for 12 to 15 minutes. The flat breads will make 8 to 12 servings, depending on whether you used the recipe for a 1-pound loaf (8 servings) or a 1½-pound loaf (12 servings).

HOME-STYLE OAT BRAN BREAD

MAKES ONE 1-POUND (8 SLICES) OR 1 1/2-POUND LOAF (12 SLICES)

Oat bran is the outer covering of the hulled oat and a favorite source of fiber for many Heartlanders. Although not the cure-all of health problems as originally claimed, oat bran is a delicious way to add fiber and makes this bread a wholesome way to start the day.

If you like a sweet bread, add your favorite finely chopped dried fruit along with the rolled oats (¼ cup for a 1-pound loaf and ⅓ cup for a 1½-pound loaf).

1-POUND LOAF	1½-POUND LOAF
¾ cup spring water (75 to 80°F)	1¼ cups spring water (75 to 80°F)
1½ cups white bread flour	2 cups white bread flour
¼ cup whole wheat flour	½ cup whole wheat flour
3 tablespoons oat bran	¼ cup oat bran
1 tablespoon nonfat dry milk	1½ tablespoons nonfat dry milk
1 teaspoon salt	1½ teaspoons salt
1½ tablespoons butter, at room temperature	2 tablespoons butter, at room temperature
1 tablespoon honey	1½ tablespoons honey
1 teaspoon rapid-rise yeast or 2 teaspoons active dry yeast	2 teaspoons rapid-rise yeast or 1 tablespoon active dry yeast
⅓ cup quick-cooking or regular rolled oats, uncooked	½ cup quick-cooking or regular rolled oats, uncooked

RECIPE WORKS BEST ON REGULAR BAKE CYCLE

1. Put all ingredients except rolled oats in the bread pan and assemble the bread machine according to manufacturer's instructions.
2. Select regular, rapid, or delayed bake cycle and light crust setting.
3. Set aside 1 tablespoon oats. After the first beep or towards the end of the first knead, add the remaining oats, following your bread machine's instructions for raisin bread. For decoration, sprinkle the reserved oats on top of the loaf after the final rise. Bake and cool as directed.

1 slice: 138 calories, 5 g protein, 3 g total fat (1.6 g saturated), 24 g carbohydrates, 294 mg sodium, 6 mg cholesterol, 2 g dietary fiber

HERB BUTTERS

MAKES 1 ⅓ CUPS

PREP TIME: 5 MINUTES

The making of herb butters dates back to the Middle Ages when blocks of butter were wrapped in scented herb leaves and stored in crocks of salted water.

The basic technique for making herb butter is simple. First cream the butter, preferably unsalted, until it is light and fluffy. Then add finely minced fresh herb leaves (a few seconds in a food processor or blender makes the chopping easy) and herb flowers, plus a smidgeon of lemon juice or grated lemon rind along with salt, pepper, and other optional seasonings as desired.

You can pack the soft butter into pretty wooden butter molds, candy molds, or small earthenware crocks. Shape chilled butter into little balls with wooden butter paddles, make curls with a butter curler, use small cookie or canape cutters to make interesting shapes, or roll the chilled butter between two pieces of waxed paper into logs or blocks.

Cover the butter in plastic wrap and chill for several hours to allow the flavors to blend. Stored in the refrigerator, herb butters should be used within three days. If frozen, herb butters will keep for 6 months.

BASIC HERB BUTTER RECIPE

- ½ pound (2 sticks) unsalted butter, at room temperature
- 5 tablespoons finely chopped fresh herbs and/or herb flowers (see suggested combinations) or 5 teaspoons dried herbs, crumbled
- 1 teaspoon fresh lemon juice or ¼ teaspoon grated lemon rind
  Salt and white pepper, to taste
  Dry mustard or paprika or cayenne pepper, to taste (optional)
  Minced garlic or shallots (optional)

ADD AS DESIRED

cumin, caraway, or poppy seeds; or sun-dried tomatoes

SUGGESTED HERB COMBINATIONS

- mint, chives, and flat-leaf parsley
- basil, tarragon, chervil, and thyme
- tarragon and shallots
- chives, parsley, tarragon, chervil, and shallots
- rosemary, chives, parsley, and garlic
- salad burnet, chives, and parsley
- chives and sun-dried tomatoes
- mint, parsley, and garlic

1. In a large bowl, using the high speed of an electric mixer or by hand, cream butter until light and fluffy. Stir in finely minced herbs and lemon juice or lemon rind. Season to taste with salt, pepper, and other desired seasonings.
2. Shape as desired. Chill or freeze.

1 tablespoon: 78 calories, 0 protein, 9 g total fat (5.5 g saturated), 0 carbohydrates, 1 mg sodium, 24 mg cholesterol, 0 dietary fiber

HONEY WALNUT BREAD

MAKES ONE 1-POUND (8 SLICES) OR 1 1/2-POUND LOAF (12 SLICES)

One bite and you'll be hooked on this bread. Delicious toasted, it's also the perfect bread for the peanut butter and jelly sandwich of your childhood.

More than half of the nation's honey is produced in the Heartland — primarily in the states of Iowa, Minnesota, and Wisconsin. Although the region produces buckwheat, soybean, and alfalfa honey, most of the honey comes from bees dining on clover.

1-POUND LOAF	1 ½-POUND LOAF
¾ cup spring water (75 to 80°F)	1 cup plus 2 tablespoons spring water (75 to 80°F)
2 cups white bread flour	3 cups white bread flour
1 tablespoon nonfat dry milk	2 tablespoons nonfat dry milk
2½ tablespoons clover honey	¼ cup clover honey
1 teaspoon salt	1½ teaspoons salt
2 teaspoons walnut oil	1 tablespoon walnut oil
1 teaspoon rapid-rise yeast or 2 teaspoons active dry yeast	2 teaspoons rapid-rise yeast or 1 tablespoon active dry yeast
½ cup coarsely chopped walnuts	¾ cup coarsely chopped walnuts

RECIPE WORKS BEST ON REGULAR BAKE CYCLE

1. Put all ingredients except walnuts in the bread pan and assemble the bread machine according to manufacturer's instructions.

2. Select regular, rapid, or delayed bake cycle and light crust setting.

3. After the first beep or towards the end of the first knead, add the walnuts, following your bread machine's instructions for raisin bread. Bake and cool as directed.

1 slice: 184 calories, 5 g protein, 7 g total fat (0.7 g saturated), 28 g carbohydrates, 273 mg sodium, 0 cholesterol, 1 g dietary fiber

MAYTAG BLUE CHEESE BREAD

MAKES ONE 1-POUND (8 SLICES) OR 1 1/2-POUND LOAF (12 SLICES)

A rich and creamy cheese riddled with deep blue veins, Maytag Blue Cheese has been made in the small community of Newton, Iowa, since 1941. Its flavor is similar, but sharper, than Roquefort or Stilton and adds a rich flavor to bread.

Use this bread, thinly sliced and lightly buttered, for tea sandwiches or canapes — topped with sprigs of watercress and peeled steamed shrimp, thin slices of cucumber and fresh dill, sliced red radishes and chopped chives, or slices of avocado and crumbled bacon.

1-POUND LOAF	1 ½-POUND LOAF
⅔ cup spring water (75 to 80°F)	1 cup spring water (75 to 80°F)
2 tablespoons dry sherry	3 tablespoons dry sherry
2 cups white bread flour	3 cups white bread flour
2 teaspoons sugar	1 tablespoon sugar
1 teaspoon salt	1½ teaspoons salt
½ teaspoon dried onion flakes	¾ teaspoon dried onion flakes
2 teaspoons butter, at room temperature	1 tablespoon butter, at room temperature
1 teaspoon rapid-rise yeast or 2 teaspoons active dry yeast	2 teaspoons rapid-rise yeast or 1 tablespoon active dry yeast
3 ounces Maytag Blue Cheese, crumbled	5 ounces Maytag Blue Cheese, crumbled
1 teaspoon freshly cracked pepper	2 teaspoons freshly cracked pepper
¼ cup chopped pecans	⅓ cup chopped pecans

RECIPE NOT APPROPRIATE FOR DELAYED BAKE CYCLE

1. Put all ingredients except blue cheese, pepper, and pecans in the bread pan and assemble the bread machine according to manufacturer's instructions.

2. Select regular or rapid bake cycle and light crust setting.

3. After the first beep or towards the end of the first knead, add the blue cheese, pepper, and pecans, following your bread machine's instructions for raisin bread. Bake and cool as directed.

1 slice: 182 calories, 6 g protein, 7 g total fat (3.0 g saturated), 23 g carbohydrates, 428 mg sodium, 11 mg cholesterol, 1 g dietary fiber

OLD-FASHIONED RAISIN LOAF

MAKES ONE 1-POUND (8 SLICES) OR 1 1/2-POUND LOAF (12 SLICES)

Nowadays, raisins are readily available and inexpensive, unlike during the pioneer times when raisins were considered a precious commodity. Everyone loves homemade raisin bread for morning toast, but it's also wonderful for lunch with peanut butter or spread with a mild goat cheese for dessert to accompany fresh fruit.

You may serve the bread unfrosted, but the lemon frosting is worth making. If you don't have dry buttermilk on hand, you can use fresh cultured low-fat (65%) buttermilk in place of the water, omitting the baking soda, as long as you aren't using the delayed bake cycle. ▶

OLD-FASHIONED RAISIN LOAF *(see previous page for photo and notes)*

1 - POUND LOAF

- ¾ cup spring water (75 to 80°F)
- 2 cups white bread flour
- 1½ tablespoons dry buttermilk
- ¼ teaspoon baking soda
- 1 tablespoon sugar
- ½ teaspoon salt
- 1½ tablespoons butter, at room temperature
- 1 large egg
- ½ teaspoon ground cinnamon
- 1½ teaspoons rapid-rise yeast
  or 2 teaspoons active dry yeast
- ⅔ cup dark seedless raisins, plumped in boiling water for 15 minutes and drained

LEMON FROSTING

- 1 cup sifted confectioners' sugar
- 1 tablespoon fresh lemon juice

1 ½ - POUND LOAF

- 1¼ cups spring water (75 to 80°F)
- 3 cups white bread flour
- 2 tablespoons dry buttermilk
- ½ teaspoon baking soda
- 1½ tablespoons sugar
- 1 teaspoon salt
- 2 tablespoons butter, at room temperature
- 1 large egg
- 1 teaspoon ground cinnamon
- 2 teaspoons rapid-rise yeast
  or 1 tablespoon active dry yeast
- 1 cup dark seedless raisins, plumped in boiling water for 15 minutes and drained

LEMON FROSTING

- 1½ cups sifted confectioners' sugar
- 4 teaspoons fresh lemon juice

RECIPE NOT APPROPRIATE FOR DELAYED BAKE CYCLE

1. Put all ingredients except raisins and frosting in the bread pan and assemble the bread machine according to manufacturer's instructions.
2. Select regular or rapid back cycle and light crust setting.
3. After the first beep or towards the end of the first knead, add the raisins, following your bread machine's instructions for raisin bread. Bake and cool as directed.
4. **Prepare Lemon Frosting:** Combine confectioners' sugar and lemon juice, beating until smooth. Spoon on top of the cooled loaf, allowing the frosting to run down the sides.

1 slice (frosted): 234 calories, 5 g protein, 4 g total fat (1.8 g saturated), 46 g carbohydrates, 214 mg sodium, 33 mg cholesterol, 1 g dietary fiber
1 slice (unfrosted): 185 calories, 5 g protein, 4 g total fat (1.8 g saturated), 34 g carbohydrates, 214 mg sodium, 33 mg cholesterol, 1 g dietary fiber

ORANGE NUT BREAD

MAKES ONE 1-POUND (8 SLICES) OR 1 1/2-POUND LOAF (12 SLICES)

Chock full of nuts with an intoxicating hint of orange, this bread will soon become a family favorite. For a lovely late afternoon treat, serve it with whipped cream cheese and a bottle of dry white wine.

Today, we take oranges for granted, but they were a precious fruit in the earlier days of the Heartland. My mother told stories of her excitement in finding an orange in her Christmas stocking — a very special treat that had been ordered months ahead from California. Depending on where you live, hazelnuts are known by another name — filberts.

1-POUND LOAF	1 ½-POUND LOAF
¾ cup spring water (75 to 80°F)	1 cup plus 2 tablespoons spring water (75 to 80°F)
2 cups white bread flour	3 cups white bread flour
1 teaspoon salt	1½ teaspoons salt
1 tablespoon nonfat dry milk	2 tablespoons nonfat dry milk
⅛ teaspoon ground nutmeg	¼ teaspoon ground nutmeg
1 tablespoon butter, at room temperature	1½ tablespoons butter, at room temperature
1 tablespoon dark rum	2 tablespoons dark rum
2 tablespoons honey	3 tablespoons honey
1 teaspoon rapid-rise yeast or 2 teaspoons active dry yeast	2 teaspoons rapid-rise yeast or 1 tablespoon active dry yeast
¼ cup chopped hazelnuts	⅓ cup chopped hazelnuts
¼ cup chopped pecans	⅓ cup chopped pecans
2 tablespoons grated orange rind	3 tablespoons grated orange rind

RECIPE WORKS BEST ON REGULAR BAKE CYCLE

1. Put all ingredients except hazelnuts, pecans, and grated orange rind in the bread pan and assemble the bread machine according to manufacturer's instructions.

2. Select regular, rapid, or delayed bake cycle and light crust setting.

3. After the first beep or towards the end of the first knead, add the hazelnuts, pecans, and grated orange rind, following your bread machine's instructions for raisin bread. Bake and cool as directed.

1 slice: 187 calories, 5 g protein, 7 g total fat (1.4 g saturated), 27 g carbohydrates, 287 mg sodium, 4 mg cholesterol, 1 g dietary fiber

PANETTONE

During the Christmas holiday, scores of Midwesterners celebrate the season with baked goods of their ethnic heritage. This citrus-flavored buttery bread is a traditional favorite of Venetians, likely to be found in Italian bakeries and homes around Chicago's north side. The bread making machine forms the bread's tall, rustic shape perfectly.

To make the gumdrop holly, roll out large green gum drops in granulated sugar to about ⅛-inch thick. Using a sharp knife, cut out holly shapes. Place on the panettone, adding candied red hots for the berries. See photograph on page 7 for decorating ideas.

1-POUND LOAF

- ¾ cup spring water (75 to 80°F)
- 2 cups white bread flour
- 1½ tablespoons nonfat dry milk
- ¾ teaspoon salt
- 3 tablespoons butter, at room temperature
- 2 large egg yolks
- ½ teaspoon grated lemon rind
- 1½ teaspoons vanilla extract
- 1½ teaspoons rapid-rise yeast
  or 2 teaspoons active dry yeast
- ½ cup finely chopped candied orange peel
- 3 tablespoons whole blanched almonds, coarsely chopped

GLAZE

- ½ cup sifted confectioners' sugar
- 1 teaspoon finely grated orange rind
- 1 tablespoon fresh orange juice

1½-POUND LOAF

- 1 cup plus 2 tablespoons spring water (75 to 80°F)
- 3 cups white bread flour
- 2 tablespoons nonfat dry milk
- 1 teaspoon salt
- 5 tablespoons butter, at room temperature
- 3 large egg yolks
- ¾ teaspoon grated lemon rind
- 2 teaspoons vanilla extract
- 2 teaspoons rapid-rise yeast
  or 1 tablespoon active dry yeast
- ¾ cup finely chopped candied orange peel
- ¼ cup whole blanched almonds, coarsely chopped

GLAZE

- ½ cup sifted confectioners' sugar
- 1 teaspoon finely grated orange rind
- 1 tablespoon fresh orange juice

RECIPE NOT APPROPRIATE FOR DELAYED BAKE CYCLE

1. Put all ingredients except candied orange peel, almonds, and glaze in the bread pan and assemble the bread machine according to manufacturer's instructions.

2. Select regular or rapid bake cycle and light crust setting.

3. After the first beep or towards the end of the first knead, add the candied orange peel and almonds, following your bread machine's instructions for raisin bread. Bake and cool as directed.

4. Prepare glaze by mixing together the confectioners' sugar, grated orange rind, and orange juice. Stir until smooth. Drizzle over the cooled panettone. If desired, decorate with gumdrop holly.

1 slice: 246 calories, 6 g protein, 8 g total fat (3.4 g saturated), 38 g carbohydrates, 253 mg sodium, 65 mg cholesterol, 1 g dietary fiber

PIZZA DOUGH

Chicago is famous for its deep-dish pizza, made easy with a bread making machine. Invented by Ike Sewell, a soldier returning to his job at Chicago's Pizzeria Uno at the end of World War II in 1943, deep-dish pizza was patterned after a flat bread topped with tomatoes that he'd eaten while stationed in Italy.

Today there are several thousand pizza parlors in the greater Chicago area serving their imitation of Ike's deep-dish pizza and more than 150 Pizzeria Uno's in twenty-five U.S. states (including eight Heartland states), the District of Columbia, Puerto Rico, and Canada serving the original recipe.

If you prefer a thin-crust pizza, feel free to bake it that way.

1 - P O U N D D O U G H	1 ½ - P O U N D D O U G H
¾ cup spring water (75 to 80°F)	1 cup plus 2 tablespoons spring water (75 to 80°F)
2 cups white bread flour	3 cups white bread flour
2 teaspoons sugar	1 tablespoon sugar
¾ teaspoon salt	1 teaspoon salt
1½ tablespoons olive oil	2 tablespoons olive oil
1 teaspoon rapid-rise yeast	2 teaspoons rapid-rise yeast
or 2 teaspoons active dry yeast	or 1 tablespoon active dry yeast
Vegetable cooking spray	Vegetable cooking spray
2 teaspoons cornmeal	1 tablespoon cornmeal

RECIPE NOT APPROPRIATE FOR DELAYED BAKE CYCLE

1. Put all ingredients except vegetable cooking spray and cornmeal in the bread pan and assemble the bread machine according to manufacturer's instructions.

2. Select dough or manual cycle.

3. When the machine beeps or manual cycle is completed, remove the bread pan and turn dough out onto a lightly floured work surface. Form dough into a round and let rest for 10 minutes.

4. For 1-pound dough: Lightly spray one 10-inch metal cake pan for deep-dish pizza (or 14-inch pizza pan for thin-crust pizza) with vegetable cooking spray. Sprinkle bottom and side of pan with 2 teaspoons cornmeal.

For 1½-pound dough: Lightly spray one 14-inch deep-dish pizza pan (or two 12-inch pizza pans for thin-crust pizza) with vegetable cooking spray. Sprinkle bottom and sides of pan(s) with 1 tablespoon cornmeal.

5. With your hands, gently stretch dough to fit evenly into the pan(s), pressing the dough halfway up the sides of the pan for the deep-dish pizza pan (forming an edge crust for the thin-crust pizza pans).

6. Select topping variation of your choice and bake as directed (see pages 74 through 77).

PIZZA TOPPINGS

FRESH TOMATO, BASIL, AND CHEESE PIZZA

Makes one 10-inch deep-dish or 14-inch thin-crust pizza (about 6 servings) or one 14-inch deep-dish or two 12-inch thin-crust pizzas (about 9 servings)

1 10-INCH DEEP-DISH PIZZA OR 1 14-INCH THIN-CRUST PIZZA	1 14-INCH DEEP-DISH PIZZA OR 2 12-INCH THIN-CRUST PIZZAS
1 tablespoon olive oil	1½ tablespoons olive oil
⅓ cup freshly grated Parmesan cheese	½ cup freshly grated Parmesan cheese
3 large plum tomatoes, thinly sliced	5 large plum tomatoes, thinly sliced
1 small yellow onion, thinly sliced	1 medium yellow onion, thinly sliced
2 large garlic cloves, thinly sliced	3 large garlic cloves, thinly sliced
½ cup shredded mozzarella cheese	¾ cup shredded mozzarella cheese
¼ cup chopped fresh basil	⅓ cup chopped fresh basil

1. Brush pizza crust with olive oil. Sprinkle with Parmesan cheese to within ½ inch from edge. Top with sliced tomatoes, onion, and garlic. Sprinkle with mozzarella. Cover and let pizza stand for 15 minutes.

2. Meanwhile, preheat oven to 500°F. Bake on bottom rack of oven until edge of crust is browned and crisp, about 20 to 25 minutes for deep-dish and 10 to 12 minutes for thin-crust pizza. Remove from oven and sprinkle with chopped basil.

1 serving: 261 calories, 10 g protein, 11 g total fat (3.3 g saturated), 33 g carbohydrates, 412 mg sodium, 12 mg cholesterol, 2 g dietary fiber

MORE PIZZA TOPPINGS

BARBECUED CHICKEN PIZZA

Makes one 10-inch deep-dish or 14-inch thin-crust pizza (about 6 servings)
or one 14-inch deep-dish or two 12-inch thin-crust pizzas (about 9 servings)

1 10-INCH DEEP-DISH PIZZA OR 1 14-INCH THIN-CRUST PIZZA

- 1 6-ounce boneless and skinless chicken breast
- 1½ teaspoons olive oil
- ⅓ cup bottled barbecue sauce
- ¼ teaspoon dried oregano leaves
- ¼ cup shredded Swiss cheese
- ¾ cup shredded mozzarella cheese
- 1 small red onion, chopped (½ cup)
- 1 small green bell pepper, seeded and chopped (½ cup)
- 4 button mushrooms, sliced (⅓ cup)

1 14-INCH DEEP-DISH PIZZA OR 2 12-INCH THIN-CRUST PIZZAS

- 1 9-ounce boneless and skinless chicken breast
- 1 tablespoon olive oil
- ½ cup bottled barbecue sauce
- ½ teaspoon dried oregano leaves
- ½ cup shredded Swiss cheese
- 1 cup shredded mozzarella cheese
- 1 medium red onion, chopped (¾ cup)
- 1 medium green bell pepper, seeded and chopped (¾ cup)
- 6 button mushrooms, sliced (½ cup)

1. Cut chicken breast in 2-inch chunks. In a large skillet, sauté chicken pieces in olive oil over medium heat for 5 minutes, turning frequently to brown all sides. Drain off excess oil and place chicken in a medium bowl, along with barbecue sauce and oregano. Mix well, cover, and refrigerate for 1 hour.

2. Preheat oven to 500°F. Leaving a 1-inch edge, sprinkle dough with Swiss cheese and half of the mozzarella cheese. Top with marinated chicken with sauce, onion, bell pepper, and mushrooms. Sprinkle with remaining mozzarella cheese.

3. Bake on bottom rack of oven until edge of crust is browned and crisp, about 20 to 25 minutes for deep-dish and 10 to 12 minutes for thin-crust pizza.

1 serving: 295 calories, 16 g protein, 11 g total fat (3.6 g saturated), 34 g carbohydrates, 467 mg sodium, 32 mg cholesterol, 2 g dietary fiber

BACON PRIMAVERA PIZZA

Makes one 10-inch deep-dish or 14-inch thin-crust pizza (about 6 servings)
or one 14-inch deep-dish or two 12-inch thin-crust pizzas (about 9 servings)

1 10-INCH DEEP-DISH PIZZA OR 1 14-INCH THIN-CRUST PIZZA	1 14-INCH DEEP-DISH PIZZA OR 2 12-INCH THIN-CRUST PIZZAS
1 tablespoon olive oil	1½ tablespoons olive oil
1 cup shredded mozzarella cheese	1½ cups shredded mozzarella cheese
¼ teaspoon dried oregano leaves	½ teaspoon dried oregano leaves
6 slices bacon, crisp-cooked and crumbled	9 slices bacon, crisp-cooked and crumbled
1 small yellow onion, thinly sliced	1 medium yellow onion, thinly sliced
1 small green bell pepper, thinly sliced	1 medium green bell pepper, thinly sliced
1 large plum tomato, thinly sliced	2 medium plum tomatoes, thinly sliced

1. Brush dough with olive oil. Sprinkle with half the mozzarella cheese to within 1 inch from edge. Top with oregano, bacon, onion, bell pepper, and tomato. Sprinkle with remaining cheese. Cover and let pizza stand for 15 minutes.

2. Meanwhile, preheat oven to 500°F. Bake on bottom rack of oven until edge of crust is browned and crisp, about 20 to 25 minutes for deep-dish and 10 to 12 minutes for thin-crust pizza.

1 serving: 296 calories, 11 g protein, 14 g total fat (4.6 g saturated), 32 g carbohydrates, 443 mg sodium, 20 mg cholesterol, 2 g dietary fiber

PIZZA TOPPING VARIATIONS

In addition to the ingredients called for in my pizza recipes, pick and choose from the following to make your own great combo:

CHEESE: Cheddar, fontina, goat cheese, Gorgonzola, Maytag Blue, ricotta, smoked mozzarella, soft and dry Jack

HERBS AND SPICES: green onions, other fresh and dried herbs such as chervil, chives, marjoram, parsley, rosemary, sage, shallots, and tarragon

MEATS AND SEAFOOD: anchovies, pepperoni, prosciutto, salami, sweet or hot sausage, shrimp, tuna

VEGETABLES: artichokes, dried or fresh chiles, eggplant, snow peas, spinach, sun-dried tomatoes, zucchini or yellow summer squash, wild mushrooms

AND: capers, dried red pepper flakes, fresh ginger, pitted olives (black, green, purple), spaghetti sauce

RAISIN PUMPERNICKEL BREAD

MAKES ONE 1-POUND (8 SLICES) OR 1 1/2-POUND LOAF (12 SLICES)

Once the Germans settling in the fertile plains of the Northern Heartland planted rye, dark loaves of bread reminiscent of those of the Old Country were eaten three times a day. This dense and dark loaf packs a lot of nutrition in each slice. Its intense flavor comes from rye flour, molasses, cocoa, and instant coffee powder.

Since the flours in this bread are heavy and low in gluten, an extra knead will be required to give the bread a second chance to create a lighter loaf. Some machines have a whole grain cycle; if yours does not, you can get this extra knead after the machine has completed its first knead by stopping the machine and resetting it to start over.

Try this superb bread for breakfast toast, piled high with sliced turkey and Swiss cheese for lunch, or spread with sweet butter to accompany a thick soup for supper.

1 - POUND LOAF	1½ - POUND LOAF
¾ cup spring water (75 to 80°F)	1 cup spring water (75 to 80°F)
1 cup white bread flour	1½ cups white bread flour
½ cup stone-ground whole wheat flour	¾ cup stone-ground whole wheat flour
½ cup rye flour	¾ cup rye flour
1 tablespoon nonfat dry milk	1½ tablespoons nonfat dry milk
½ teaspoon salt	1 teaspoon salt
1½ tablespoons butter, at room temperature	2 tablespoons butter, at room temperature
2 tablespoons dark molasses	3 tablespoons dark molasses
1 tablespoon unsweetened cocoa powder	1½ tablespoons unsweetened cocoa powder
1 teaspoon instant coffee powder	1½ teaspoons instant coffee powder
1 teaspoon rapid-rise yeast or 2 teaspoons active dry yeast	2 teaspoons rapid-rise yeast or 1 tablespoon active dry yeast
½ cup dark seedless raisins	¾ cup dark seedless raisins

RECIPE NOT APPROPRIATE FOR THE RAPID OR DELAYED BAKE CYCLES

1. Put all ingredients except raisins in the bread pan and assemble the bread machine according to manufacturer's instructions.

2. Select whole grain, dough, or manual cycle and light crust setting, if available.

3. If you are using the whole grain cycle, add the raisins when the machine beeps. If you are using the dough or manual cycle, when the machine beeps or the first knead is completed, press the "stop" button. Reset the machine and start again. When the machine beeps again or towards the end of this first knead, sprinkle in the raisins.

4. Bake and cool as directed.

1 slice: 168 calories, 4 g protein, 3 g total fat (1.5 g saturated), 33 g carbohydrates, 164 mg sodium, 6 mg cholesterol, 3 g dietary fiber

ROSEMARY BREAD

MAKES ONE 1-POUND (8 SLICES) OR 1 1/2-POUND LOAF (12 SLICES)

This bread is one of my personal favorites, probably because I love rosemary. When we lived in California, I grew rosemary as ground cover and it needed a heavy hand with the pruning shears several times a year. Nowadays I am limited to pots on the patio since this wonderful herb doesn't like cold weather.

This recipe requires fresh rosemary. If you don't grow it, look for packages of fresh rosemary at your supermarket.

1-POUND LOAF	1 ½-POUND LOAF
¾ cup spring water (75 to 80°F)	1 cup plus 2 tablespoons spring water (75 to 80°F)
1¾ cups white bread flour	2⅔ cups white bread flour
¼ cup stone-ground whole wheat flour	⅓ cup stone-ground whole wheat flour
1 teaspoon salt	1½ teaspoons salt
1 tablespoon nonfat dry milk	2 tablespoons nonfat dry milk
1 tablespoon olive oil	1½ tablespoons olive oil
2 teaspoons sugar	1 tablespoon sugar
1 teaspoon rapid-rise yeast or 2 teaspoons active dry yeast	2 teaspoons rapid-rise yeast or 1 tablespoon active dry yeast
1½ tablespoons chopped fresh rosemary	2 tablespoons chopped fresh rosemary

RECIPE WORKS BEST ON REGULAR BAKE CYCLE

1. Put all ingredients except rosemary in the bread pan and assemble the bread machine according to manufacturer's instructions.

2. Select regular, rapid, or delayed bake cycle and medium crust setting.

3. After the first beep or towards the end of the first knead, add the rosemary, following your bread machine's instructions for raisin bread. Bake and cool as directed.

1 slice: 125 calories, 4 g protein, 2 g total fat (0.4 g saturated), 22 g carbohydrates, 272 mg sodium, 0 cholesterol, 1 g dietary fiber

SEED AND HONEY BREAD

MAKES ONE 1-POUND (8 SLICES) OR 1 1/2-POUND LOAF (12 SLICES)

Café Latte is a renowned bakery-cafe in St. Paul, Minnesota, which grinds its own wheat every day to use in their fabulous breads and pastries.

Several years ago, a friend returning from St. Paul brought me a loaf of their famous Dakota Bread, a very dense bread filled with crunchy seeds. The recipe was developed by Christen Gilbertson who named the bread after her home state of South Dakota.

This is an adaptation of her recipe for bread making machines. If you've been making 100% whole wheat bread in your machine, you will already have the gluten in your pantry. If not, you'll find it at a natural foods store, along with the seeds needed for this recipe.

1-POUND LOAF	1 ½-POUND LOAF
¾ cup plus 1 tablespoon spring water (75 to 80°F)	1¼ cups plus 1 tablespoon spring water (75 to 80°F)
1½ cups white bread flour	2 cups white bread flour
½ cup whole wheat flour	¾ cup whole wheat flour
¼ cup cracked wheat	½ cup cracked wheat
1 teaspoon salt	1½ teaspoons salt
2 tablespoons honey	3 tablespoons honey
2 teaspoons gluten	1 tablespoon gluten
1 tablespoon mild vegetable oil, such as canola	1½ tablespoons mild vegetable oil, such as canola
1 teaspoon rapid-rise yeast or 2 teaspoons active dry yeast	2 teaspoons rapid-rise yeast or 1 tablespoon active dry yeast
¼ cup raw pumpkin seeds	⅓ cup raw pumpkin seeds
½ cup raw sunflower seeds	⅔ cup raw sunflower seeds
2 teaspoons sesame seeds	1 tablespoon sesame seeds
2 teaspoons poppy seeds	1 tablespoon poppy seeds

RECIPE NOT APPROPRIATE FOR RAPID OR DELAYED BAKE CYCLES

1. Put all ingredients except the seeds in the bread pan and assemble the bread machine according to manufacturer's instructions.

2. Select whole grain cycle, dough, or manual cycle and light crust setting, if available.

3. Finely chop 8 of the pumpkin seeds; set aside. Add the remaining pumpkin seeds, sunflower seeds, sesame seeds, and poppy seeds after the beep or towards the end of the first knead, following your bread machine's instructions for raisin bread. For added crunch, sprinkle the chopped pumpkin seeds on top of the loaf after the final rise.

4. Bake and cool as directed.

1 slice: 223 calories, 8 g protein, 8 g total fat (0.9 g saturated), 32 g carbohydrates, 271 mg sodium, 0 cholesterol, 4 g dietary fiber

SWEDISH LIMPA

MAKES ONE 1-POUND (8 SLICES)
OR 1 1/2-POUND LOAF (12 SLICES)

Sold at bakeries throughout much of the Heartland, this delightful rye bread is easily made in the bread machine. The use of anise, caraway, and fennel seeds gives this loaf a flavor unique to Scandinavian baking that distinguishes limpa from other rye breads.

1 - P O U N D L O A F	1 ½ - P O U N D L O A F
¾ cup spring water (75 to 80°F)	1 cup plus 2 tablespoons spring water (75 to 80°F)
1¼ cups white bread flour	1¾ cups white bread flour
¾ cup rye flour	1¼ cups rye flour
1 tablespoon dry nonfat milk	2 tablespoons dry nonfat milk
1½ tablespoons butter, at room temperature	2 tablespoons butter, at room temperature
2 teaspoons dark brown sugar	1 tablespoon dark brown sugar
1½ tablespoons dark molasses	1 tablespoon dark molasses
1 teaspoon salt	1½ teaspoons salt
1 teaspoon rapid-rise yeast or 2 teaspoons active dry yeast	2 teaspoons rapid-rise yeast or 1 tablespoon active dry yeast
¼ tcaspoon anise seeds	½ teaspoon anise seeds
¼ teaspoon caraway seeds	½ teaspoon caraway seeds
½ teaspoon fennel seeds	½ teaspoon fennel seeds
2 teaspoons grated orange rind	1 tablespoon grated orange rind

RECIPE NOT APPROPRIATE FOR DELAYED BAKE CYCLE

1. Put all ingredients except seeds and grated orange rind in the bread pan and assemble the bread machine according to manufacturer's instructions.
2. Select regular or rapid bake cycle and light crust setting.
3. After the first beep or towards the end of the first knead, add the seeds and orange rind, following your bread machine's instructions for raisin bread. Bake and cool as directed.

1 slice: 135 calories, 4 g protein, 3 g total fat (1.5 g saturated), 24 g carbohydrates, 295 mg sodium, 6 mg cholesterol, 2 g dietary fiber

SWEET POTATO BREAD

MAKES ONE 1-POUND (8 SLICES) OR 1 1/2-POUND LOAF (12 SLICES)

This will become one of your favorite breads for fall. Not too sweet, the loaf is a lovely pale orange color. The same bread could also be made with a wide assortment of winter squash — acorn, butternut, sugar pumpkin, striped turban, or Blue Hubbard — with equal success.

1-POUND LOAF

- ½ cup spring water (75 to 80°F)
- 2 cups white bread flour
- 1½ tablespoons nonfat dry milk
- ½ teaspoon salt
- 1½ tablespoons butter, at room temperature
- 2 teaspoons pure maple syrup
- 2 teaspoons dark brown sugar
- ⅓ cup plain cooked mashed sweet potato or yam potato, at room temperature
- 1 tablespoon orange liqueur, such as Grand Marnier
- 1 teaspoon grated orange rind
- 1 teaspoon rapid-rise yeast or 2 teaspoons active dry yeast

1 ½-POUND LOAF

- ¾ cup spring water (75 to 80°F)
- 3 cups white bread flour
- 2 tablespoons nonfat dry milk
- 1 teaspoon salt
- 2 tablespoons butter, at room temperature
- 1 tablespoon pure maple syrup
- 1 tablespoon dark brown sugar
- ½ cup cold cooked mashed sweet potato or yam potato, at room temperature
- 1½ tablespoons orange liqueur, such as Grand Marnier
- 1½ teaspoons grated orange rind
- 2 teaspoons rapid-rise yeast or 1 tablespoon active dry yeast

RECIPE WORKS BEST ON REGULAR OR DELAYED BAKE CYCLE

1. Put ingredients in the bread pan and assemble the bread machine according to manufacturer's instructions.

2. Select regular, rapid, or delayed bake cycle and light crust setting.

3. Bake and cool as directed.

1 slice: 148 calories, 4 g protein, 3 g total fat (1.5 g saturated), 26 g carbohydrates, 164 mg sodium, 6 mg cholesterol, 1 g dietary fiber

TOMATO BREAD

MAKES ONE 1-POUND (8 SLICES)
OR 1 1/2-POUND LOAF (12 SLICES)

Thanks to sun-dried tomatoes, you can make this bread, redolent of summer, any time of year. I can buy sun-dried tomatoes in bulk at my supermarket. If you're using sun-dried tomatoes that are not packed in olive oil, you'll need to soften them first in warm water for about 30 minutes.

1-POUND LOAF	1½-POUND LOAF
¾ cup spring water (75 to 80°F)	1 cup plus 2 tablespoons spring water (75 to 80°F)
2 cups white bread flour	3 cups white bread flour
3 tablespoons nonfat dry milk	¼ cup nonfat dry milk
2 teaspoons brown sugar	1 tablespoon brown sugar
1 teaspoon salt	1½ teaspoons salt
1½ tablespoons butter, at room temperature	2 tablespoons butter, at room temperature
1 teaspoon rapid-rise yeast or 2 teaspoons active dry yeast	2 teaspoons rapid-rise yeast or 1 tablespoon active dry yeast
⅓ cup snipped sun-dried tomatoes (packed in oil), well drained	½ cup snipped sun-dried tomatoes (packed in oil), well drained
¾ teaspoon dried basil leaves	1 teaspoon dried basil leaves

RECIPE NOT APPROPRIATE FOR DELAYED BAKE CYCLE

1. Put all ingredients except sun-dried tomatoes and basil in the bread pan and assemble the bread machine according to manufacturer's instructions.
2. Select regular or rapid bake cycle and medium crust setting.
3. After the first beep or towards the end of the first knead, add the sun-dried tomatoes and basil, following your bread machine's instructions for raisin bread. Bake and cool as directed.

1 slice: 150 calories, 5 g protein, 4 g total fat (1.7 g saturated), 24 g carbohydrates, 324 mg sodium, 6 mg cholesterol, 1 g dietary fiber

WALNUT BEER BREAD

MAKES ONE 1-POUND (8 SLICES) OR 1 1/2-POUND LOAF (12 SLICES)

Heartlanders often use beer in their cooking, especially in the states of Wisconsin and Missouri. Beer and native black walnuts give this soft textured country loaf a heady flavor and fragrance. Serve this with Blue Cheese Spread (page 33) and fresh pears, apples, or grapes for a casual dessert.

It's also excellent for breakfast, spread with whipped cream cheese and sprinkled with freshly grated orange rind.

To release the natural gases from the beer for this recipe, pour the beer back and forth between two glasses until it no longer forms a foamy head, or pour the beer into a shallow container and let it set at room temperature for about 30 minutes.

1 - P O U N D L O A F	1 ½ - P O U N D L O A F
1 cup flat beer, at room temperature	1¼ cups flat beer, at room temperature
1½ cups white bread flour	2 cups white bread flour
¼ cup rye flour	½ cup rye flour
¼ cup whole wheat flour	½ cup whole wheat flour
1½ tablespoons nonfat dry milk	2 tablespoons nonfat dry milk
1 tablespoon light brown sugar	1½ tablespoons light brown sugar
½ teaspoon salt	1 teaspoon salt
1½ tablespoons butter, at room temperature	2 tablespoons butter, at room temperature
1 teaspoon rapid-rise yeast	2 teaspoons rapid-rise yeast
or 2 teaspoons active dry yeast	or 1 tablespoon active dry yeast
½ cup chopped black walnuts	⅔ cup chopped black walnuts
⅓ cup golden raisins	½ cup golden raisins

RECIPE NOT APPROPRIATE FOR DELAYED BAKE CYCLE

1. Put all ingredients except black walnuts and raisins in the bread pan and assemble the bread machine according to manufacturer's instructions.

2. Select regular or rapid bake cycle and medium crust setting.

3. After the first beep or towards the end of the first knead, add the black walnuts and raisins, following your bread machine's instructions for raisin bread. Bake and cool as directed.

1 slice: 209 calories, 6 g protein, 7 g total fat (1.8 g saturated), 30 g carbohydrates, 165 mg sodium, 6 mg cholesterol, 2 g dietary fiber

T O M A T O   J A M

M A K E S   1   C U P

PREP TIME: 10 MINUTES • COOK TIME: 35 TO 40 MINUTES

1 pound ripe plum tomatoes	⅔ cup sugar
¼ teaspoon crushed dried hot pepper flakes	6 tablespoons cider vinegar
	½ teaspoon salt
½ teaspoon pickling spices	¼ teaspoon freshly ground pepper

1. Bring a large saucepan of water to a boil. Add tomatoes and cook for 2 minutes. Drain and plunge tomatoes into a bowl of ice water to stop the cooking process. Peel the tomatoes and drain on paper towels. Finely chop tomatoes.

2. Place the hot pepper flakes and pickling spices in a 6-inch square of cheesecloth. Tie with kitchen string to form a spice bag.

3. In a heavy saucepan, combine tomatoes, spice bag, and remaining ingredients. Slowly bring to a boil. Reduce heat and simmer, uncovered, stirring frequently, for 30 minutes. (The jam will be quite thick — the consistency of a chunky chutney.)

4. Remove from heat and discard spice bag. Allow tomato jam to cool. Spoon into sterilized glass jars and refrigerate. Use within one week. (This recipe can be easily doubled or tripled.)

1 tablespoon: 39 calories, 0 protein, 0 total fat, 10 g carbohydrates, 69 mg sodium, 0 cholesterol, trace dietary fiber

WILD RICE AND WHEAT BREAD

MAKES ONE 1-POUND (8 SLICES) OR 1 1/2-POUND LOAF (12 SLICES)

The wild rice of Minnesota's lake country is harvested in late August and early September. This bread's a perfect way to celebrate!

Bake this special loaf early in the day to serve warm for breakfast with freshly squeezed orange juice and a wedge of honeydew melon.

1-POUND LOAF	1½-POUND LOAF
¾ cup spring water (75 to 80°F)	1 cup plus 2 tablespoons spring water (75 to 80°F)
1¾ cups white bread flour	2½ cups white bread flour
¼ cup whole wheat flour	½ cup whole wheat flour
1 tablespoon nonfat dry milk	1½ tablespoons nonfat dry milk
1 tablespoon sugar	1½ tablespoons sugar
1 teaspoon salt	1½ teaspoons salt
1½ tablespoons butter, at room temperature	2 tablespoons butter, at room temperature
1 large egg	1 large egg
¾ cup cooked wild rice	1 cup cooked wild rice
1 teaspoon rapid-rise yeast or 2 teaspoons active dry yeast	2 teaspoons rapid-rise yeast or 1 tablespoon active dry yeast
1 tablespoon sesame seeds	1½ tablespoons sesame seeds

RECIPE NOT APPROPRIATE FOR DELAYED BAKE CYCLE

1. Put all ingredients except sesame seeds in the bread pan and assemble the bread machine according to manufacturer's instructions.

2. Select regular or rapid bake cycle and light crust setting.

3. After the first beep or towards the end of the first knead, add the sesame seeds, following your bread machine's instructions for raisin bread. Bake and cool as directed.

1 slice: 162 calories, 6 g protein, 4 g total fat (1.8 g saturated), 26 g carbohydrates, 303 mg sodium, 32 mg cholesterol, 1 g dietary fiber

YEASTED CORN BREAD

MAKES ONE 1-POUND (8 SLICES) OR 1 1/2-POUND LOAF (12 SLICES)

You'll love this one! It has a nice chewy texture and smells wonderful baking. More substantial than quick corn bread, it's the perfect accompaniment to spicy soups and stews.

Many millers in the Heartland have returned to grindstone milling so stone-ground cornmeal shouldn't be hard to find. You can always use regular cornmeal, but the bread will have a finer texture. Whether you use white or yellow cornmeal is your choice.

If you don't have dry buttermilk, you can replace the water with fresh cultured low-fat (1.5%) buttermilk as long as you aren't using the delayed bake cycle.

1-POUND LOAF	1½-POUND LOAF
¾ cup plus 2 tablespoons spring water (75 to 80°F)	1½ cups spring water (75 to 80°F)
2 cups white bread flour	2⅔ cups white bread flour
⅔ cup stone-ground cornmeal	1 cup stone-ground cornmeal
3 tablespoons dry buttermilk	¼ cup dry buttermilk
¼ teaspoon baking soda	½ teaspoon baking soda
2 teaspoons sugar	1 tablespoon sugar
1 teaspoon salt	1½ teaspoons salt
1 tablespoon olive oil	1½ tablespoons olive oil
1½ teaspoons rapid-rise yeast or 2 teaspoons active dry yeast	2 teaspoons rapid-rise yeast or 1 tablespoon active dry yeast

RECIPE NOT APPROPRIATE FOR DELAYED BAKE CYCLE IF USING FRESH BUTTERMILK

1. Put ingredients in the bread pan and assemble the bread machine according to manufacturer's instructions.
2. Select regular, rapid, or delayed bake cycle and medium crust setting.
3. Bake and cool as directed.

1 slice: 175 calories, 6 g protein, 3 g total fat (0.5 g saturated), 32 g carbohydrates, 323 mg sodium, 2 mg cholesterol, 2 g dietary fiber

QUICK BREADS

ASY TO MAKE AND SO VERSATILE, quick breads are very popular in the Heartland, where bread is considered an essential part of most every meal. Made possible by the discovery of two leavening agents — baking soda (bicarbonate of soda) and baking powder (a combination of baking soda, an acid such as cream of tartar, and a moisture-absorber such as cornstarch) — during the nineteenth century, quick breads were made fresh for most every meal. Mixed and ready to bake in minutes, quick breads need no rising time.

When I was growing up in Kansas, we lived many miles from the nearest grocery store. If my mother had nothing that I wanted for lunch, she would take down her butterscotch-colored crockery bowl and I knew we were having fresh muffins. Spread with sweet butter and some of her homemade jam, those "make-do" lunches were pure heaven.

Muffins are a quick batter bread — the batter category includes sweet loaves (or tea breads), corn breads, coffee cakes, waffles, pancakes, and popovers (the latter leavened by steam rather than baking soda or baking powder). These quick batter breads must be baked in a mold, such as muffin tins or loaf pans, as the batter is too thin to hold its own shape. The second category is quick dough breads, such as biscuits, scones, Irish soda breads, and shortcakes. They will hold their shape and are baked directly on a baking sheet or pan.

Most of my recipes are heavily laden with fruits and nuts to make them moist and sweet. Quick breads are delectable served warm or at room temperature. The loaves should be cooled for at least 5 to 10 minutes before slicing. Quick breads keep well and, with the exception of popovers, can be refrigerated or frozen for later use. Wrap the baked, cooled bread airtight in plastic wrap and refrigerate for up to a week. To freeze, place the quick bread in a second wrap of aluminum foil or a plastic freezer bag and freeze for up to three months.

Most of my muffin recipes call for standard (2¾-inch diameter) muffin cups. For a special brunch, you might want to bake miniature muffins (1⅝-inch diameter) — it'll take 10 to 15 minutes at 375°F. To bake giant or oversized muffins (3- to 3¼-inch diameter), increase the baking time to 25 to 30 minutes at 375°F.

The secret to a biscuit or scone that's crisp on the outside, tender and flaky on the inside, is a fast, gentle touch. Handle the dough as little as possible, patting or rolling the dough on a lightly floured work surface. Press the floured cutter down firmly with a downward motion. To reroll the scraps, press the dough together with your fingers, keeping the height of the dough the same as the original dough. You can make square or diamond-shaped biscuits and scones by cutting the dough with a chef's knife into a straight-sided grid (you won't have any scraps to reroll).

With these recipes in hand, you will have an invaluable collection of easy-to-do recipes for extraordinary quick breads.

CHEDDAR CHEESE DROP BISCUITS *(see previous page for photo and notes)*

2 cups unbleached all-purpose flour
½ teaspoon salt
1 tablespoon baking powder
½ teaspoon baking soda
6 tablespoons (¾ stick) cold butter, cut into 6 pieces

1 cup shredded sharp Cheddar cheese (4 ounces)
1 cup lowfat (1.5%) buttermilk

PREP TIME: 15 MIN
BAKE TIME: 10–12 MIN

1. Preheat oven to 450°F. Lightly grease a baking sheet.
2. In a large bowl, combine flour, salt, baking powder, and baking soda. Using a pastry blender or two knives, cut in butter until mixture resembles coarse crumbs. Stir in cheese. Add buttermilk all at once, stirring until dry ingredients are just moistened.
3. Drop dough by heaping tablespoons onto prepared baking sheet in 8 round clumps approximately 3 inches in diameter and about 2 inches apart. Bake for 10 to 12 minutes, until golden.

1 biscuit: 260 calories, 8 g protein, 14 g total fat (8.5 g saturated), 26 g carbohydrates, 603 mg sodium, 39 mg cholesterol, 1 g dietary fiber

SWEET DESSERT BISCUIT VARIATION

Substitute ¼ cup of sugar for the Cheddar cheese. Mix and bake as above. Split and layer with fresh fruit as you would a shortcake. Top with fresh whipped cream, if desired.

CLOUD BISCUITS

MAKES 20 BISCUITS

A restaurant landmark in Wichita, Kansas, for more than 30 years, Elizabeth's Tea Room was famous for their biscuits. Baked close together in a metal tin that had been generously greased with solid shortening, they were as light as a cloud.

These little gems are also light, but much lower in fat. They are hard to resist right out of the oven with nothing more than a smidgeon of sweet butter.

2   cups unbleached all-purpose flour
1   tablespoon plus 1 teaspoon baking powder
1   tablespoon sugar
½   teaspoon salt

½   cup (1 stick) cold butter, cut into 8 pieces
⅔   cup half-and-half
1   large egg, slightly beaten with 1 tablespoon whole milk

PREP TIME: 20 MIN
BAKE TIME: 10–12 MIN

1. Preheat oven to 450°F. Lightly oil a 9-inch metal cake pan.
2. In a large bowl, combine flour, baking powder, sugar, and salt. Using a pastry blender or two knives, cut in butter until mixture resembles coarse crumbs.
3. Make a well in the center and add the half-and-half. Stir with a fork until mixture holds together. Transfer to a floured surface and knead gently. Do not overmix.
4. Pat or roll to a ½-inch thickness. Cut with a biscuit cutter into twenty 2-inch rounds. Place in prepared pan, arranging biscuits so that they are touching. Brush biscuits with egg mixture. Bake for 10 to 12 minutes, until golden brown.

1 biscuit: 104 calories, 2 g protein, 6 g total fat (3.6 g saturated), 11 g carbohydrates, 205 mg sodium, 26 mg cholesterol, trace dietary fiber

CARROT BREAD

MAKES 1 LOAF (10 SERVINGS)

I've been making this family recipe for years. If you want to give it as a gift from your kitchen, bake the batter in two smaller (3½ x 5-inch) pans, decreasing the baking time by 20 minutes.

1½ cups unbleached all-purpose flour
2 teaspoons baking powder
1 teaspoon ground cinnamon
½ teaspoon baking soda
½ teaspoon ground nutmeg
½ teaspoon salt
⅓ cup broken pecans, toasted
(see below)

2 large eggs
1 cup sugar
⅔ cup mild vegetable oil, such as canola
1 tablespoon fresh lemon juice
1½ cups shredded carrots
(about 4 medium carrots)
1 cup water-packed canned pineapple
bits, drained

**PREP TIME:
20 MIN
BAKE TIME:
35–40 MIN
COOL TIME:
5 MIN**

1. Preheat oven to 350°F. Lightly grease an 8½ x 4½-inch loaf pan. Onto wax paper, sift together flour, baking powder, cinnamon, baking soda, nutmeg, and salt. Toss with the pecans.
2. In a large bowl, whisk together eggs and sugar until thick and light colored. Gradually whisk in the oil and lemon juice. Stir in flour mixture, then fold in the carrots and pineapple. Stir just until evenly moistened. Do not overmix.
3. Spoon mixture into prepared pan and bake for 35 to 40 minutes, until lightly brown and a tester comes out clean when inserted in the center.
4. Cool in pan for 5 minutes. Remove from pan and cool on a rack.

1 slice: 338 calories, 4 g protein, 18 g total fat (1.6 g saturated), 41 g carbohydrates, 286 mg sodium, 43 mg cholesterol, 2 g dietary fiber

TOASTING NUTS

Toasting brings out the flavor of pecans and other nuts. Spread pecans in a single layer on a baking sheet and toast in a 350°F oven for 3 to 5 minutes, until golden brown and fragrant, shaking the pan once or twice. Be careful not to over-toast.

CHOCOLATE BREAD

MAKES 1 BREAD (12 SERVINGS)

If someone you love adores chocolate or macadamia nuts, try this bread. The combination is fantastic and makes for a very special morning or afternoon treat. Try this bread spread with cream cheese.

In earlier days, chocolate was used in ice cream, pudding, or cake for special occasions only, like someone's birthday. These days, however, chocolate has become a popular addition to bread, muffins, biscuits, and scones.

3 cups unbleached all-purpose flour
½ cup sugar
1 tablespoon baking powder
1 teaspoon baking soda
6 ounces imported semi-sweet dark chocolate, cut into small chunks

½ cup chopped macadamia nuts
1¾ cups lowfat (1.5%) buttermilk
2 large eggs
3 tablespoons butter, melted
½ teaspoon vanilla extract

**PREP TIME:
20 MIN**
**BAKE TIME:
45 MIN**
**COOL TIME:
5 MIN**

1. Preheat oven to 350°F. Grease a 10-inch springform pan with removable bottom.

2. In a large bowl, mix together flour, sugar, baking powder, baking soda, chocolate chunks, and macadamia nuts.

3. In a small bowl, whisk buttermilk, eggs, 2 tablespoons of the melted butter, and vanilla extract. Beat well. Make a well in the center of the flour mixture. Add buttermilk mixture and stir just until evenly moistened. Do not overmix. Spoon batter into prepared pan.

4. Drizzle with remaining 1 tablespoon butter. Bake for 5 minutes. Using a knife, swirl through batter several times to distribute chocolate. Bake for 40 minutes more, or until lightly browned and bread pulls away from the sides of the pan. Let cool in pan for 5 minutes. Remove from pan and cool on a rack. Serve warm or at room temperature.

1 serving: 311 calories, 7 g protein, 13 g total fat (2.8 g saturated), 43 g carbohydrates, 305 mg sodium, 44 mg cholesterol, 1 g dietary fiber

FRESH PEAR BREAD

MAKES 1 LOAF (12 SERVINGS)

This bread gets a jumpstart with a packaged biscuit and baking mix, but it does need some time to rise since it also contains yeast. If you're watching fat grams, use 1% lowfat milk, a reduced fat baking mix, and 1 whole egg plus 2 egg whites.

The pear brandy used to soak the raisins makes this bread very special, but regular brandy could also be used.

½ cup golden raisins
¼ cup pear brandy
1 package (¼ ounce) rapid-rise yeast
2 tablespoons confectioners' sugar
1 cup warm whole milk, about 110° F
2 large eggs, slightly beaten

3¾ cups biscuit and baking mix
¼ teaspoon salt
¼ teaspoon cream of tartar
2 medium fresh Bartlett or Bosc pears
1 tablespoon fresh lemon juice

**PREP TIME:
20 MIN + 30 MIN
FOR RISING**

**BAKE TIME:
50–55 MIN**

**COOL TIME:
5 MIN**

1. In a small bowl, soak raisins in brandy for 15 minutes. Set aside.

2. In another small bowl, sprinkle yeast and 1 teaspoon confectioners' sugar over milk and stir until yeast dissolves completely. Let stand until foamy, about 5 minutes. Stir in eggs.

3. Meanwhile, in a large bowl, combine biscuit and baking mix, remaining confectioners' sugar, salt, and cream of tartar.

4. Peel, core, and chop pears. Sprinkle with lemon juice. Make a well in the center of the flour mixture. Pour in yeast mixture and undrained raisins. Stir just until dry ingredients are evenly moistened. Fold in pears. Cover and let rise in a warm place until doubled in bulk, about 30 minutes.

5. While dough is rising, preheat oven to 350° F and lightly oil a 9 x 5 x 3-inch loaf pan. Stir down bread dough. Spoon dough into prepared pan. Bake for 50 to 55 minutes, until golden brown and a tester inserted near the center comes out clean. Cool for 5 minutes. Remove from pan and cool on a rack. Serve warm or at room temperature.

1 serving: 242 calories, 5 g protein, 7 g total fat (1.9 g saturated), 38 g carbohydrates, 545 mg sodium, 39 mg cholesterol, 2 g dietary fiber

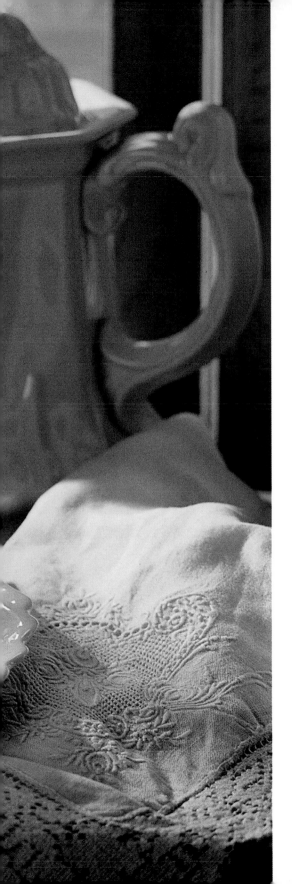

LEMON TEA BREAD

MAKES 2 LOAVES (10 SERVINGS EACH)

This recipe is adapted from one used years ago by the Kansas State University Student Union dining room for faculty teas and special luncheons. It's very lemony and quite delicious!

- 3 cups all-purpose flour
- 3¾ teaspoons baking powder
- 1 teaspoon salt
- 1 cup chopped, toasted walnuts (see page 99)
- 4 large eggs
- 2¼ cups sugar
- 1 cup plus 2 tablespoons mild vegetable oil, such as canola
- 3 tablespoons grated lemon rind
- 1 cup plus 2 tablespoons cup whole milk
- 6 tablespoons (¾ stick) butter, melted

LEMON GLAZE
- ½ cup fresh lemon juice
- 2 tablespoons grated lemon rind
- ¾ cup sugar

PREP TIME:
20 MIN
BAKE TIME:
50–60 MIN
COOL TIME:
10 MIN

1. Preheat oven to 350°F. Grease and flour two 8½ x 4½-inch loaf pans.

2. Onto wax paper, sift together flour, baking powder, and salt; toss with walnuts. In a large bowl of an electric mixer, or by hand, beat eggs on medium speed until frothy. Add sugar, oil, and lemon rind. Continue to beat on medium speed for 2 minutes.

3. Mixing by hand, stir in flour mixture, one-third at a time, alternating with milk, beginning and ending with the flour mixture. Do not overmix. Stir in melted butter.

4. Divide batter between prepared pans. Bake for 50 to 60 minutes, until golden and a tester inserted near the center comes out clean.

5. Meanwhile, in a small bowl, combine glaze ingredients, stirring until sugar dissolves. Leaving loaves in pans, use a long skewer to poke numerous holes all the way to bottom of loaf. Drizzle glaze over hot loaves. Cool bread in pans on a rack for 10 minutes or until glaze soaks into bread; turn out onto racks and let cool completely.

1 serving: 388 calories, 5 g protein, 21 g total fat (4.0 g saturated), 47 g carbohydrates, 254 mg sodium, 54 mg cholesterol, 1 g dietary fiber

RHUBARB STREUSEL BREAD

MAKES 1 LOAF (12 SERVINGS)

Rhubarb is a standard in the Heartland vegetable garden. Though we think of rhubarb as a fruit, botanically, it's a vegetable. The tart, cherry red stalks make a fabulous bread that's perfect for teatime or morning coffee.

1½ cups unbleached all-purpose flour
1 teaspoon baking powder
½ teaspoon salt
1 large egg
¾ cup sugar
⅓ cup mild vegetable oil, such as canola
½ cup whole milk
½ teaspoon lemon extract

1 cup chopped uncooked fresh rhubarb

STREUSEL TOPPING
¼ cup chopped pecans
¼ cup sugar
1 tablespoon grated lemon rind
1 tablespoon butter, at room temperature

PREP TIME: 20 MIN
BAKE TIME: 50–55 MIN
COOL TIME: 5 MIN

1. Preheat oven to 350°F. Grease a 9 x 5 x 3-inch loaf pan.

2. Onto wax paper, sift together flour, baking powder, and salt. In a large bowl, whisk egg until frothy. Add sugar and oil, mixing well. Whisk in the milk and lemon extract. Fold in the flour mixture. Gently stir in rhubarb. Spoon batter into prepared pan.

3. **Prepare Streusel Topping:** Combine ingredients in a small bowl, tossing with a fork. Sprinkle over batter.

4. Bake for 50 to 55 minutes, until a tester inserted near the center comes out clean. Cool in pan on a rack for 5 minutes. Turn loaf out onto the rack.

1 serving: 215 calories, 3 g protein, 10 g total fat (1.5 g saturated), 30 g carbohydrates, 150 mg sodium, 22 mg cholesterol, 1 g dietary fiber

SHERRIED CRANBERRY ORANGE BREAD

MAKES 1 LOAF (12 SERVINGS)

This exceptional bread is not overly rich, yet it's wonderfully moist and scrumptious. Keep fresh cranberries in the freezer so you can make this bread any time. You can also use dried cranberries if you soak them first in the sherry. This bread freezes well, so make an extra loaf to serve in the summertime with ice tea.

2 cups unbleached all-purpose flour	3 tablespoons dry sherry
1 cup sugar	2 tablespoons butter, melted
½ teaspoon salt	½ cup chopped, toasted walnuts (see page 99)
½ teaspoon baking soda	1 cup chopped fresh cranberries
½ cup fresh orange juice	1½ tablespoons grated orange rind

PREP TIME: 20 MIN
BAKE TIME: 55 MIN
COOL TIME: 5 MIN

1. Preheat oven to 325°F. Lightly grease an 8½ x 4½-inch loaf pan.

2. In a large bowl, combine flour, sugar, salt, and baking soda. In a medium bowl, whisk together the orange juice, sherry, and butter.

3. Make a well in the center of the flour mixture and pour in orange juice mixture. Stir until dry ingredients are evenly moistened. Do not overmix. Fold in walnuts, cranberries, and orange rind. Spoon into prepared pan and smooth top.

4. Bake for 55 minutes, until lightly browned and a tester inserted near the center comes out clean.

5. Cool in pan for 5 minutes. Remove bread from pan and cool on a rack.

1 serving: 201 calories, 3 g protein, 5 g total fat (1.5 g saturated), 36 g carbohydrates, 162 mg sodium, 5 mg cholesterol, 1 g dietary fiber

STRAWBERRY BREAD

MAKES 1 LOAF (12 SERVINGS)

We grew a huge patch of strawberries on our suburban ranch when I was growing up in Wichita. I wish my mother had known how to make this luscious bread. It's the perfect way to celebrate spring.

1⅔ cups unbleached all-purpose flour
¾ cup sugar
1 teaspoon ground cinnamon
½ teaspoon salt
½ teaspoon baking soda

⅔ cup chopped, toasted pecans, optional (see page 99)
2 large eggs
½ cup mild vegetable oil, such as canola
1 cup fresh strawberries, hulled and thinly sliced

1. Preheat oven to 350°F. Butter and flour a 9 x 5 x 3-inch loaf pan.
2. In a large bowl, combine flour, sugar, cinnamon, salt, and baking soda. Toss with pecans, if desired. In another bowl, whisk eggs until frothy; whisk in oil.
3. Make a well in the center of the flour mixture. Pour in the egg mixture and stir until dry ingredients are just evenly moistened. Do not overmix. Fold in strawberries.
4. Spoon batter into prepared pan and smooth top. Bake for 45 to 50 minutes, until a tester inserted near the center comes out clean. Let cool in pan for 5 minutes. Remove from pan and cool on rack.

PREP TIME:
20 MIN
BAKE TIME:
45–50 MIN
COOL TIME:
5 MIN

1 serving: 252 calories, 3 g protein, 15 g total fat (1.3 g saturated), 28 g carbohydrates, 152 mg sodium, 35 mg cholesterol, 1 g dietary fiber

SWEET CORN SKILLET BREAD

MAKES 1 BREAD (12 SERVINGS)

This is a fluffy corn bread spiked with Mexican spices and kernels of corn. Cut into thick wedges and serve with herb butter or Tomato Jam. Preheat the greased skillet in the oven (as they do in the South) to give the corn bread a crusty bottom.

1¼ cups stone-ground yellow cornmeal
1¼ cups unbleached all-purpose flour
3 tablespoons sugar
1 tablespoon plus 1 teaspoon baking powder
1 teaspoon ground chili powder
1 teaspoon ground cumin

1 teaspoon salt
6 tablespoons (¾ stick) cold butter, cut into 6 pieces
2 large eggs, slightly beaten
1⅔ cups whole milk
1 cup fresh corn kernels or frozen corn kernels, thawed and drained

PREP TIME:
15 MIN
BAKE TIME:
30 MIN
COOL TIME:
5 MIN

1. Preheat oven to 400°F. Grease a 10-inch ovenproof skillet or 9-inch square baking pan. Preheat in oven for 5 minutes
2. In a large bowl, mix together cornmeal, flour, sugar, baking powder, chili powder, cumin, and salt.
3. Using a pastry blender or two knives, cut in butter until mixture resembles coarse crumbs. Add eggs and milk, stirring just until dry ingredients are evenly moistened. Do not overmix. Stir in corn kernels.
4. Spread batter in prepared pan. Bake until deep golden, about 30 minutes. Let cool in pan on a rack for 5 minutes. Remove from pan. Serve hot or at room temperature.

1 serving: 207 calories, 5 g protein, 8 g total fat (4.6 g saturated), 29 g carbohydrates, 430 mg sodium, 56 mg cholesterol, 2 g dietary fiber

SEE
HERB BUTTERS
PAGE 64
TOMATO JAM
PAGE 87

TOASTED PECAN BANANA BREAD

MAKES 1 LOAF (12 SERVINGS)

My mother used to buy overripe bananas at the supermarket to make banana bread. The bananas were very sweet and just right for baking. A swirl of cream cheese through the bread adds a special flavor.

2 cups unbleached all-purpose flour
2 teaspoons baking powder
½ teaspoon baking soda
½ cup toasted pecans, coarsely chopped (see page 99)
5 tablespoons butter, at room temperature
¾ cup sugar
2 large eggs

3 medium ripe bananas, mashed (1⅓ cups)
1 teaspoon grated lemon rind

CREAM CHEESE FILLING
6 ounces cream cheese, at room temperature
⅓ cup sugar
1 large egg
½ teaspoon vanilla extract

PREP TIME:
25 MIN
BAKE TIME:
55 MIN–1 HR
COOL TIME:
5 MIN

1. Preheat oven to 350°F. Grease a 9 x 5 x 3 -inch loaf pan.
2. Onto wax paper, sift together the flour, baking powder, and baking soda. Toss with pecans.
3. In a large bowl, using an electric mixer on medium speed, or by hand, cream together butter and sugar. Beat in eggs, one at a time. Mixing by hand, stir in bananas and lemon rind. Add the flour mixture, stirring until evenly moistened. Do not overmix.
4. **Prepare Cream Cheese Filling:** In a food processor or blender, place all ingredients and process until smooth.
5. Spoon two-thirds of the batter into prepared pan. Top with filling, then remaining batter. Lightly swirl with a knife. Bake for 55 minutes to 1 hour, or until golden brown and a tester inserted near the center comes out clean. If bread browns too quickly, loosely cover with a sheet of aluminum foil. Cool in pan on a rack for 5 minutes. Remove from pan.

1 serving: 316 calories, 6 g protein, 15 g total fat (6.8 g saturated), 42 g carbohydrates, 241 mg sodium, 82 mg cholesterol, 2 g dietary fiber

SEE
TOASTING NUTS
PAGE 99

WALNUT-FIG BREAD

MAKES 1 LOAF (12 SERVINGS)

From mid-September through late October, it's harvest time for the Heartland's nut crop. Besides walnuts (black and English), the Midwestern states also grow butternuts, chestnuts, hazelnuts (sometimes called filberts), hicans (a cross between a hickory nut and a pecan), hickory nuts, and pecans. This quick bread can be made with either black walnuts or English walnuts. It's particularly wonderful toasted and spread with Lemon Marmalade (page 112). ▶

WALNUT-FIG BREAD *(see previous page for photo and notes)*

¼ cup boiling water
¾ cup chopped dried figs
2 cups unbleached all-purpose flour
2 teaspoons baking powder
½ teaspoon salt
6 tablespoons (¾ stick) butter at
   room temperature
¾ cup sugar

2 large eggs
1 tablespoon grated orange rind
1 cup whole milk
½ cup chopped, toasted walnuts
   (see page 99)

SUGAR TOPPING
2 tablespoons sugar
1 tablespoon grated orange rind

**PREP TIME:
25 MIN

BAKE TIME:
55 MIN-1 HR

COOL TIME:
5 MIN**

1. Preheat oven to 325°F. Grease an 8½ x 4½-inch loaf pan.
2. In a small bowl, pour boiling water over dried figs. Let soften for 5 minutes; drain.
3. Onto wax paper, sift together flour, baking powder, and salt.
4. In a large bowl, using an electric mixer on medium speed, or by hand, cream together butter and sugar. Beat in eggs, one at a time, beating well after each addition.
5. Mixing by hand, stir in grated orange rind. Stir flour mixture into egg mixture, one-third at a time, alternating with milk, beginning and ending with the flour mixture. Do not overmix. Fold in walnuts and figs.
6. Spoon batter into prepared pan. Combine topping ingredients and sprinkle on top of batter. Bake for 55 minutes to 1 hour, or until golden brown and a tester inserted near the center comes out clean. Cool in pan for 5 minutes. Remove from pan.

1 serving: 267 calories, 5 g protein, 11 g total fat (4.6 g saturated), 39 g carbohydrates, 251 mg sodium, 54 mg cholesterol, 2 g dietary fiber

LEMON MARMALADE

MAKES 1 PINT

PREP TIME: 10 MIN • COOK TIME: 40 MIN

5 large lemons, sliced in paper-thin slices
3 cups water
2¼ cups sugar

1. In a large saucepan, combine lemon slices and water. Cook over medium heat until lemon slices are tender, about 20 minutes, stirring occasionally.
2. Remove from heat. Strain liquid from fruit into a quart measuring cup, leaving lemons in the saucepan. Add enough water to the measuring cup to make 3 cups liquid. Return to saucepan with the sugar.
3. Bring to a full rolling boil over high heat. Boil rapidly, uncovered, stirring frequently, for 15 to 20 minutes, until mixture thickens or a candy thermometer registers 8° higher than the boiling point of water at your altitude. Stir and skim off foam that forms on the surface. Cool. Transfer to a sterilized glass jar, seal, and store in the refrigerator for up to 3 weeks.

1 tablespoon: 58 calories, 0 protein, 0 total fat, 15 g carbohydrates, 0 sodium, 0 cholesterol, trace dietary fiber

APPLE BUTTER

MAKES 2 ½ PINTS

PREP TIME: 5 MIN • COOK TIME: ABOUT 2 HR

4 pounds cooking apples, such as Ida Red, Jonathan, or Macoun
4 cups sweet apple cider
1 cup sugar

1. Rinse, core, and quarter apples; do not peel. Put apples and cider in a large, heavy saucepan. Bring to a boil over medium-high heat. Reduce heat, cover, and simmer for 30 minutes.
2. Using a slotted spoon, remove apples and cool briefly before removing and discarding the peelings. Leave apple cider in the pan. In a food processor or blender, purée apples for 10 seconds. Set aside.
3. Meanwhile, continue to simmer apple cider, uncovered, until reduced by half, or until you have about 1½ cups cider. Return puréed apples to saucepan. Simmer, uncovered, for 30 minutes, stirring occasionally.
4. Stir in sugar and return to a boil. Reduce heat and continue to simmer, uncovered, stirring frequently, until mixture resembles thick applesauce (the apple butter will further thicken as it cools), about 45 to 55 minutes.
5. Remove from heat and ladle into sterilized jars. Wipe rims well and seal. Let stand at room temperature for 24 hours. If seals are not tight, refrigerate and use within 3 weeks.

1 tablespoon: 26 calories, 0 protein, 0 total fat, 7 g carbohydrates, 0 sodium, 0 cholesterol, trace dietary fiber

QUINCE JELLY

MAKES 1 ½ PINTS

PREP TIME: 10 MIN • COOK TIME: 30 MIN

1 pound fresh quince, peeled and cored
2 cups water
1½ cups sugar
3 tablespoons fresh lemon juice
1 teaspoon grated lemon rind

1. In a small saucepan over low heat, combine all ingredients. Cook, stirring occasionally, until quince is soft, about 30 minutes.
2. Using a fork, partially mash mixture, leaving some chunks of quince. Transfer to sterilized glass jars, wipe the rims well, seal, and refrigerate for up to 2 weeks.

1 tablespoon: 28 calories, 0 protein, 0 total fat. 7 g carbohydrates, 0 sodium, 0 cholesterol, 0 dietary fiber

WHEAT SODA BREAD

MAKES 1 LOAF (10 SERVINGS)

I created this recipe by accident. I had wanted to make Irish soda bread for St. Patrick's Day, but found I only had whole wheat flour and no regular whole milk. This delicious result proves that good recipes often are born by forced substitution.

2½ cups whole wheat flour
½ teaspoon salt
1 teaspoon baking soda

1¼ cup lowfat (1.5 %) buttermilk
1 large egg
2 tablespoons honey

**PREP TIME:
15 MIN
BAKE TIME:
20–25 MIN
COOL TIME:
10 MIN**

1. Preheat oven to 375°F. Line a baking sheet with parchment paper.

2. In a large bowl, combine flour, salt, and soda. In a medium bowl, whisk together buttermilk, egg, and honey. Make a well in the center of the flour mixture and pour in the buttermilk mixture. Stir just until dry ingredients are evenly moistened. Do not overmix.

3. On a lightly floured work surface, shape dough into an 8-inch round loaf. Place on prepared baking sheet and bake for 20 to 25 minutes, or until nicely browned. Cool on a rack for 10 minutes before slicing.

1 serving: 134 calories, 6 g protein, 1 g total fat (0.4 g saturated), 27 g carbohydrates, 273 mg sodium, 22 mg cholesterol, 3 g dietary fiber

SPRING FRUIT JAM

MAKES 2 PINTS

PREP TIME: 20 MIN • COOK TIME: 1¼ HR

1 pound fresh rhubarb
1 pint fresh strawberries
1 10-ounce can crushed pineapple, undrained
1 cup light corn syrup
3 cups sugar
¼ cup fresh lemon juice
1 tablespoon grated lemon rind

1. Peel rhubarb; cut into ½-inch pieces. Wash and hull strawberries; coarsely chop.

2. In a large saucepan over medium heat, combine rhubarb, strawberries, and remaining ingredients. Bring to a full rolling boil, stirring constantly. Reduce heat and cook, uncovered, stirring occasionally until mixture is thick, about 1 hour, or until a candy thermometer registers 8° above the boiling temperature of water at your altitude.

3. Transfer mixture to sterilized glass jars, wipe the rims well, seal, and refrigerate for up to 3 weeks.

1 tablespoon: 56 calories, 0 protein, 0 total fat, 15 g carbohydrates, 7 mg sodium, 0 cholesterol, 0 g dietary fiber

FRESH BLUEBERRY COFFEE CAKE

MAKES 16 SERVINGS

My sister-in-law Ruth, a native of Missouri, used to make this coffee cake for the morning meetings of her church women's society. I added fresh blueberries and the results are spectacular. Take this to the office to serve with coffee.

2 cups unbleached all-purpose flour	2 cups fresh blueberries, picked over, rinsed and dried on paper towels
1 teaspoon baking powder	STREUSEL TOPPING
½ teaspoon baking soda	⅓ cup firmly packed light brown sugar
½ teaspoon salt	¼ cup granulated sugar
5 tablespoons butter, at room temperature	1 teaspoon ground cinnamon
1 cup sugar	1 cup chopped, toasted pecans, optional (see page 99)
3 large eggs	
1 teaspoon vanilla extract	
1 cup sour cream	

**PREP TIME:
25 MIN**

**BAKE TIME:
50–55 MIN**

**COOL TIME:
10 MIN**

1. Preheat oven to 350°F. Grease a 9-inch Bundt pan.
2. In a medium bowl, combine flour, baking powder, baking soda, and salt. In a large bowl, using an electric mixer on medium speed, or by hand, cream together butter and sugar. Beat in eggs, one at a time, beating well after each addition. Stir in vanilla extract.
3. Mixing by hand, stir the flour mixture into the sugar-egg mixture, one-third at a time, alternating with sour cream, beginning and ending with the dry ingredients. Do not overmix.
4. **Prepare Streusel Topping:** In a small bowl, combine all of the topping ingredients. Spoon half of the batter into the prepared pan. Sprinkle with half of the blueberries and half of the topping. Cover with remaining batter and the remaining blueberries. Sprinkle with remaining topping.
5. Bake for 10 minutes. Insert a table knife in the batter with the tip pointing downward. Gently cut through the batter in a circular pattern several times. Continue to bake for another 40 to 45 minutes, until a tester inserted in the center comes out clean. Let cool in the pan on a rack for 10 minutes. Loosen edges and remove from pan by holding plate upside down on top of pan and inverting cake onto plate. Serve warm.

1 serving: 266 calories, 4 g protein, 13 g total fat (4.8 g saturated), 35 g carbohydrates, 195 mg sodium, 56 mg cholesterol, 1 g dietary fiber

AUNT RUTH'S DAINTY SPICE ROLLS

MAKES ABOUT 24 ROLLS

For more than 60 years, my aunt Ruth was regarded as one of the best cooks in Garden City, Kansas. She made these little rolls every time I went to visit her.

2 to 2¼ cups unbleached all-purpose flour
2 tablespoons sugar
1 tablespoon plus 1 teaspoon baking powder
1 teaspoon salt
½ cup (1 stick) cold butter, cut into 8 pieces
1 cup whole milk
2 large eggs, slightly beaten

RAISIN FILLING

½ cup seedless raisins
¼ cup sugar
½ teaspoon ground cinnamon
¼ teaspoon ground nutmeg
⅛ teaspoon ground cloves
¼ cup (½ stick) butter, melted
1 large egg yolk, beaten with 1 teaspoon water

PREP TIME: 35 MIN

BAKE TIME: 15–20 MIN

1. Preheat oven to 400°F. Lightly grease a baking sheet.
2. In a large bowl, sift together flour, sugar, baking powder, and salt.
3. Using a pastry blender or two knives, cut in butter until mixture resembles fine crumbs. In a small bowl, whisk together milk and eggs. Stir into flour-butter mixture just until a soft dough forms. Do not overmix.
4. Turn dough out onto a lightly floured work surface. Roll out to ¼-inch thickness and using a sharp knife cut into twenty-four 3-inch squares.
5. **Prepare Raisin Filling:** In a food processor, combine raisins, sugar, cinnamon, nutmeg, and cloves. Pulse until finely chopped. Brush each square with melted butter and sprinkle with 1½ teaspoons Raisin Filling. Roll up each square jelly-roll fashion and press edges together to seal. Place 2 inches apart on prepared baking sheet, seam side down, and brush each roll with egg yolk mixture. Bake for 15 to 20 minutes, or until golden brown. Transfer to a rack. Serve hot or warm.

1 roll: 132 calories, 2 g protein, 7 g total fat (4.0 g saturated), 16 g carbohydrates, 240 mg sodium, 43 mg cholesterol, 1 g dietary fiber

APPLE-BRAN MUFFINS

MAKES 12 MUFFINS

A rich muffin, chock full of fresh apples, oats, and bran, that provides a nourishing boost on frosty mornings. Assemble the dry ingredients the night before; then chop the apples, mix the batter, and bake the muffins the next morning so they're piping hot for the breakfast table.

1½ cups unbleached all-purpose flour	½ cup chopped, toasted pecans (see page 99)
2 teaspoons baking powder	½ cup golden raisins
1 teaspoon ground cinnamon	2 large tart green apples, such as Granny Smith, peeled, cored, and coarsely chopped (2 cups)
½ teaspoon baking soda	1 cup lowfat (1.5%) buttermilk
½ teaspoon ground ginger	½ cup sugar
½ teaspoon ground nutmeg	⅓ cup mild vegetable oil, such as canola
1 cup dry shredded bran cereal	2 large eggs
1 cup regular or quick rolled oats, uncooked	

PREP TIME: 20 MIN
BAKE TIME: 25–30 MIN
COOL TIME: 5 MIN

1. Preheat oven to 400°F. Grease 12 standard muffin cups or line with paper liners.

2. In a large bowl, sift together flour, baking powder, cinnamon, baking soda, ginger, and nutmeg. Stir in bran and oats. Toss with pecans and raisins.

3. In a food processor or blender, combine apples, buttermilk, sugar, oil, and eggs until apples are finely chopped, about 10 seconds.

4. Make a well in the center of the dry ingredients and add the apple-buttermilk mixture, stirring just until dry ingredients are evenly moistened. Do not overmix. Spoon into prepared muffin cups, filling cups two-thirds full. Bake for 25 to 30 minutes, until golden and a tester inserted near the center comes out clean. Cool in pan on a rack for 5 minutes before removing from pan. Serve hot or warm.

1 muffin: 278 calories, 6 g protein, 11 g total fat (1.2 g saturated), 41 g carbohydrates, 168 mg sodium, 36 mg cholesterol, 3 g dietary fiber

DRIED CRANBERRY MUFFINS

MAKES 18 MUFFINS

Serve these muffins with an assortment of ripened cheeses and strong coffee for a special Continental breakfast. If you can't find dried cranberries in your supermarket or natural food store, they are available by mail-order (see Sources, page 142), or you could substitute golden raisins or chopped dried apricots.

2 cups unbleached all-purpose flour
2 teaspoons baking powder
½ teaspoon salt
6 tablespoons (¾ stick) butter, at room temperature
1¼ cups granulated sugar

2 large eggs, at room temperature
¾ cup whole milk
¾ cup dried cranberries, coarsely chopped

CINNAMON TOPPING

2 tablespoons firmly packed light brown sugar
½ teaspoon ground cinnamon

**PREP TIME:
15 MIN

BAKE TIME:
20–25 MIN

COOL TIME:
5 MIN**

1. Preheat oven to 375°F. Grease 18 standard muffin cups or line with paper liners.
2. Onto wax paper, sift together flour, baking powder, and salt.
3. In a large bowl using an electric mixer on medium speed, or by hand, cream together butter and sugar until light and fluffy. Add eggs, one at a time, beating well after each addition.
4. Mixing by hand, stir flour mixture into egg mixture, one-third at a time, alternating with milk, beginning and ending with dry ingredients. Do not overmix. Fold in cranberries. Spoon batter into prepared muffin cups, filling cups two-thirds full.

5. **Prepare Cinnamon Topping:** Combine light brown sugar and cinnamon. Sprinkle mixture over the tops of the muffins. Bake for 20 to 25 minutes, or until a tester inserted in the center comes out clean. Cool in pan on a rack for 5 minutes before removing from pan. Serve hot or warm.

1 muffin: 172 calories, 3 g protein, 5 g total fat (2.8 g saturated), 30 g carbohydrates, 165 mg sodium, 35 mg cholesterol, 1 g dietary fiber

FRESH ORANGE MUFFINS

MAKES 18 MUFFINS

These muffins are perfect for foggy, misty mornings when we could all use a little sunshine. Or, for a sweet-savory treat at afternoon tea, try them with Microwave Cranberry-Strawberry Conserve (page 18) and slices of smoked turkey.

2 cups plus 2 tablespoons cake flour	½ cup sour cream
2 teaspoons baking powder	⅔ cup fresh orange juice
½ teaspoon baking soda	3 tablespoons grated orange rind
½ teaspoon salt	STREUSEL TOPPING
6 tablespoons (¾ stick) butter, at room temperature	2 tablespoons cold butter
	2 tablespoons firmly packed light brown sugar
⅔ cup sugar	½ cup cake flour
3 large eggs	1 teaspoon ground cinnamon

PREP TIME: 20 MIN
BAKE TIME: 20–25 MIN
COOL TIME: 5 MIN

1. Preheat oven to 350°F. Grease 18 standard muffin cups or line with paper liners.

2. Onto wax paper, sift together the cake flour, baking powder, baking soda, and salt.

3. In a large bowl using an electric mixer on medium speed, or by hand, cream together butter and sugar. Add eggs, one at a time, beating well after each addition.

4. Mixing by hand, stir flour mixture into the creamed mixture, one-third at a time, alternating with sour cream and orange juice, beginning and ending with dry ingredients. Mix just until dry ingredients are evenly moistened. Do not overmix. Fold in orange rind. Spoon batter into prepared muffin cups, filling cups two-thirds full.

5. **Prepare Streusel Topping:** In a food processor or blender, combine all of the topping ingredients until mixture resembles coarse crumbs. Sprinkle topping over muffins and bake for 20 to 25 minutes, until golden brown and a tester inserted in the center comes out clean. Cool in pan on a rack for 5 minutes before removing from pan. Serve hot or at room temperature.

1 muffin: 160 calories, 3 g protein, 7 g total fat (4.3 g saturated), 21 g carbohydrates, 215 mg sodium, 52 mg cholesterol, trace dietary fiber

GINGER-PUMPKIN MUFFINS

MAKES 12 MUFFINS

These muffins fill the house with the aroma of Thanksgiving while they are baking. Make them for breakfast on that morning or anytime you crave comfort and joy!

2 cups unbleached all-purpose flour
1 tablespoon baking powder
1½ teaspoons ground ginger
½ teaspoon ground cinnamon
¼ teaspoon ground cloves
¼ teaspoon salt
⅛ teaspoon ground nutmeg
2 large eggs

½ cup sugar
½ cup mild vegetable oil, such as canola
1 cup canned pumpkin
⅔ cup canned evaporated whole milk
¼ cup sweetened flaked coconut
WALNUT TOPPING
12 walnut halves, toasted (see page 99)
2 tablespoons sugar

**PREP TIME:
15 MIN
BAKE TIME:
20–25 MIN
COOL TIME:
5 MIN**

1. Preheat oven to 375°F. Grease 12 standard muffin cups or line with paper liners.

2. Into a large bowl, sift together flour, baking powder, ginger, cinnamon, cloves, salt, and nutmeg.

3. In a medium bowl, whisk eggs until frothy. Whisk in ½ cup sugar and oil. Add pumpkin and evaporated milk, mixing well. Stir in coconut.

4. Make a well in the center of the flour mixture. Pour in egg-pumpkin mixture and stir just until dry ingredients are evenly moistened. Do not overmix. Spoon batter into prepared muffin cups, filling two-thirds full. Top each muffin with a walnut half and sprinkle with some of the 2 tablespoons sugar.

5. Bake for 20 to 25 minutes, until lightly browned and a tester inserted in the center comes out clean. Cool in pan on a rack for 5 minutes before removing from pan. Best when served hot.

1 muffin: 257 calories, 5 g protein, 13 g total fat (2.1 g saturated), 31 g carbohydrates, 198 mg sodium, 40 mg cholesterol, 2 g dietary fiber

OLD-FASHIONED PRUNE MUFFINS

MAKES 12 MUFFINS

I used to love the prune muffins that were a standard item at the coffee shop next door to my father's Wichita office. I'm sure the coffee shop is no longer there, but this lightened version brings back the memory.

In the late 1800s and early 1900s, prunes were commonly used in cakes and pies. It'll take only one bite of this muffin to realize why prunes were once prized for baked goods.

2 cups unbleached all-purpose flour
¾ cup sugar
2 teaspoons baking powder
1 teaspoon ground allspice
1 teaspoon ground cinnamon
½ teaspoon salt
6 tablespoons (¾ stick) butter, melted

1 large egg, plus 2 large egg whites
1 cup whole milk
1 teaspoon vanilla extract
12 ounces (about 1¾ cups) moist-packed pitted prunes, coarsely chopped
¾ cup chopped toasted walnuts, optional (see page 99)

PREP TIME: 15 MIN
BAKE TIME: 20-25 MIN
COOL TIME: 5 MIN

1. Preheat oven to 375°F. Lightly grease 12 standard muffin cups or line with paper liners.
2. In a large bowl, combine flour, sugar, baking powder, allspice, cinnamon, and salt.
3. In another bowl, whisk together butter, egg, egg whites, milk, and vanilla extract. Make a well in the center of the flour mixture. Pour in the milk mixture and stir until dry ingredients are evenly moistened. Do not overmix. Fold in prunes plus the walnuts, if desired.
4. Spoon batter into prepared muffin cups, filling cups two-thirds full. Bake for 20 to 25 minutes, or until lightly browned and a tester inserted in the center comes out clean. Cool in pan on a rack for 5 minutes before removing from pan. Serve hot or warm.

1 muffin: 315 calories, 6 g protein, 12 g total fat (4.6 g saturated), 49 g carbohydrates, 256 mg sodium, 36 mg cholesterol, 4 g dietary fiber

PERSIMMON WALNUT MUFFINS

MAKES 12 MUFFINS

My parents knew where persimmons grew wild in the Ozarks, near Branson, Missouri. In the fall, we'd combine a day of fishing with a persimmon picking for delectable results.

The persimmons imported from South America in the spring and early summer have a high water content and are not as suitable for baking as the Midwestern persimmons. Fortunately, you can buy persimmon pulp by mail-order (see Sources, page 142). The black walnuts are also available by mail-order or you can substitute English walnuts.

2	to 3 large ripe persimmons	½	cup black walnuts, coarsely chopped
2½	cups unbleached all-purpose flour	3	large eggs
1	tablespoon baking powder	½	cup sugar
½	teaspoon ground allspice	⅔	cup whole milk
½	teaspoon ground cinnamon	⅓	cup walnut oil
½	teaspoon salt		

PREP TIME: 25 MIN
BAKE TIME: 20–25 MIN
COOL TIME: 5 MIN

1. Preheat oven to 400°F. Grease 12 standard muffin cups or line with paper liners.

2. Cut persimmons in half and remove seeds. Using a spoon, scoop out flesh and place in a food processor or blender. Purée until smooth. Measure ¾ cup purée. Set aside. (You can refrigerate any remaining purée, and mix into sour cream, plain yogurt, or a basic vinaigrette dressing for fruit salads.)

3. In a large bowl, sift together flour, baking powder, allspice, cinnamon, and salt; toss with black walnuts.

4. In another large bowl using an electric mixer on medium speed, or by hand, beat eggs until frothy. Add sugar and beat until light and fluffy, then beat in milk and oil.

5. Make a well in the center of the flour mixture. Mixing by hand, stir in persimmon purée and stir just until dry ingredients are evenly moistened. Do not overmix.

6. Spoon batter into prepared muffin cups, filling cups two-thirds full. Bake for 20 to 25 minutes, until lightly browned and a tester inserted in center comes out clean. Cool in pan on a rack for 5 minutes before removing from pan. Serve hot or warm.

CHERRY JAM

MAKES 4 PINTS

PREP TIME: 15 MIN • COOK TIME: 30 MIN

3	pounds tart red cherries, washed, stemmed, and pitted
4½	cups sugar
3	tablespoons fresh lemon juice
½	teaspoon salt

1. In a medium saucepan, combine all ingredients over medium heat. Slowly bring to a boil, stirring constantly.

2. Increase heat to medium-high and cook, stirring frequently, for about 15 minutes, until mixture is slightly thickened and a candy thermometer reaches 8° above the boiling point of water at your alitutde. (The jam will thicken more as it cools.)

3. Remove from heat and spoon into hot sterilized jars. Wipe rims well and seal. Let stand at room temperature for 24 hours. If seals are not tight, refrigerate and use within 3 weeks.

1 tablespoon: 32 calories, 0 protein, 0 total fat, 8 g carbohydrates, 9 mg sodium, 0 cholesterol, 0 dietary fiber

1 muffin: 247 calories, 6 g protein, 11 g total fat (1.5 g saturated), 32 g carbohydrates, 234 mg sodium, 55 mg cholesterol, 1 g dietary fiber

QUICK PEACH MARMALADE

MAKES 4 PINTS

PREP TIME: 20 MIN • COOK TIME: 10 MIN

3	pounds fresh peaches (about 6 large peaches)
1	medium orange
7½	cups sugar
¼	cup fresh lemon juice
½	teaspoon butter
1	3-ounce pouch liquid pectin

1. Wash, peel, and pit peaches. In two or three batches, place peaches in a food processor or blender and pulse or use the on/off switch until the peaches are finely chopped but not puréed. (You should have 4 cups of peaches.) Transfer peaches and their juice to a large saucepan.

2. Wash the orange, but do not peel. Cut in half and remove any seeds. Cut each half into 4 to 6 pieces and place in a food processor or blender; finely chop but do not purée.

Add to peaches in saucepan along with the sugar, lemon juice, and butter.

3. While stirring, bring the mixture to a boil over medium heat. Boil for 1 minute, stirring constantly. Add the pectin, all at once, and stir constantly until mixture returns to a rolling boil. Cook for 1 minute more. Remove from heat and spoon into sterilized jars to within ⅛ inch of tops. Wipe rims well and seal. Let stand at room temperature for 24 hours, then refrigerate for up to 3 weeks. (Marmalade will further thicken as it chills.)

1 tablespoon: 50 calories, 0 protein, 0 total fat, 13 g carbohydrates, 0 sodium, 0 cholesterol, 0 dietary fiber

REGAL BLACKBERRY (OR BLUEBERRY) MUFFINS

MAKES 6 MUFFINS

From early July to the end of August, it's berry time throughout much of the Heartland. In all, ten kinds of berries are cultivated in the Midwest — blackberries, blueberries, cranberries, currants, elderberries, gooseberries, lingonberries, mulberries, raspberries, and strawberries.

You'll find blackberries, blueberries, cranberries, raspberries, and strawberries in the supermarket, but for the others, you'll need to locate a roadside stand, farmer's market, "you-pick" berry farm, or grow your own.

Here, blackberries or blueberries utilize the season's harvest. Bake them in giant (sometimes labeled Texas-size) muffin cups for an incredible taste treat.

1½ cups fresh blackberries or blueberries, picked over and stemmed	6 tablespoons (¾ stick) butter, at room temperature
2 cups unbleached all-purpose flour	¾ cup sugar
2 teaspoons baking powder	2 large eggs
½ teaspoon ground cinnamon	1 cup whole milk
½ teaspoon salt	

PREP TIME: 15 MIN
BAKE TIME: 20–25 MIN
COOL TIME: 5 MIN

1. Preheat oven to 375°F. Grease 6 giant (or Texas-size) 3¼-inch muffin cups or line with paper liners. Rinse berries and drain on paper towels.

2. Onto wax paper, sift together flour, baking powder, cinnamon, and salt.

3. In a large bowl using an electric mixer on medium speed, or by hand, cream together butter and sugar until light and fluffy. Beat in eggs, one at a time, beating well after each addition.

4. Mixing by hand, stir flour mixture into butter-egg mixture, one-third at a time, alternating with milk, beginning and ending with dry ingredients. Do not overmix.

5. Half-fill prepared muffin cups and sprinkle with berries. Cover with remaining batter so that it is level with the tops of cups. Bake for 20 to 25 minutes, until browned and tops spring back when gently pressed in center. Cool in pan on a rack for 5 minutes before removing from pan. Serve hot or warm.

1 muffin: 420 calories, 8 g protein, 15 g total fat (8.7 g saturated), 64 g carbohydrates, 500 mg sodium, 107 mg cholesterol, 3 g dietary fiber

SOUR CREAM RAISIN MUFFINS

MAKES 12 MUFFINS

Sour cream and raisins are found in fresh-baked pies throughout the Midwest. The combination also makes a comforting muffin. These are best served warm and fresh with sweet butter.

2 cups unbleached all-purpose flour
1½ teaspoons baking powder
1 teaspoon baking soda
½ teaspoon allspice
½ teaspoon salt
6 tablespoons (¾ stick) butter, at room temperature

¼ cup granulated sugar
¼ cup firmly packed light brown sugar
1 teaspoon vanilla extract
3 large eggs
1 cup sour cream
¾ cup dark seedless raisins

PREP TIME:
15 MIN
BAKE TIME:
20–25 MIN
COOL TIME:
5 MIN

1. Preheat oven to 375°F. Lightly grease 12 standard muffin cups or line with paper liners.

2. Onto wax paper, sift together flour, baking powder, baking soda, allspice, and salt.

3. In a large bowl, using an electric mixer on medium speed, or by hand, cream together butter, both sugars, and vanilla extract. Add eggs, one at a time, beating well after each addition.

4. Mixing by hand, gradually add flour mixture to butter mixture alternating with sour cream, one-third at a time, beginning and ending with dry ingredients and mixing until dry ingredients are evenly moistened. Do not overmix.

5. Spoon batter into prepared muffin cups, filling two-thirds full. Bake for 20 to 25 minutes, or until golden brown and a tester inserted in the center comes out clean. Cool in pan on a rack for 5 minutes before removing from pan. Serve hot or warm.

1 muffin: 246 calories, 5 g protein, 11 g total fat (6.5 g saturated), 32 g carbohydrates, 342 mg sodium, 77 mg cholesterol, 1 g dietary fiber

SWEET POTATO PECAN MUFFINS

MAKES 12 MUFFINS

Are the dark-orange sweet potatoes labeled "yams" sold in your supermarket really yams? Probably not. The potatoes are most likely mislabeled and are actually a dark variety of sweet potatoes. With the exception of a limited crop grown in Florida for specialty Latin American markets, yams are not grown in the United States for general consumption.

A true yam comes from Africa and is a member of a tropical herb family. However, more than 40 varieties of sweet potatoes, a member of the morning-glory family, are grown throughout the United States. The varieties grown in the Heartland tend to be drier and less sweet than those grown down South. If you live in the South, you may want to decrease the brown sugar slightly when making these cake-like muffins.

2½ cups unbleached all-purpose flour
2 teaspoons baking powder
1 teaspoon ground cinnamon
½ teaspoon baking soda
½ teaspoon ground ginger
¼ teaspoon ground cloves
¼ teaspoon salt
1½ cups grated, peeled sweet potato (8 ounces)

⅓ cup chopped, toasted pecans (page 99)
6 tablespoons (¾ stick) butter, at room temperature
⅔ cup firmly packed dark brown sugar
2 large eggs
1 cup whole milk
¼ cup pure maple syrup

1. Preheat oven to 375°F. Grease 12 standard muffin cups or line with paper liners.
2. In a large bowl, sift together flour, baking powder, cinnamon, baking soda, ginger, cloves, and salt. Stir in sweet potato and pecans.
3. In another bowl using an electric mixer on medium speed, or by hand, cream together butter and sugar. Add eggs, one at a time, beating well after each addition.
4. Mixing by hand, stir in milk and maple syrup. Make a well in the center of the flour mixture and pour in the egg mixture. Stir just until the dry ingredients are evenly moistened. Do not overmix.
5. Spoon batter into prepared muffin cups, filling cups two-thirds full. Bake for 20 to 25 minutes, until browned and a tester inserted in the center comes out clean. Cool in pan on a rack for 5 minutes before removing from pan. Serve hot or warm.

PREP TIME: 20 MIN
BAKE TIME: 20–25 MIN
COOL TIME: 5 MIN

1 muffin: 258 calories, 5 g protein, 10 g total fat (4.5 g saturated), 38 g carbohydrates, 295 mg sodium, 54 mg cholesterol, 2 g dietary fiber

FRESH HERB POPOVERS

MAKES 6 POPOVERS

These airy breads puff up because of the high proportion of liquid in the batter, making steam in the center as the popovers bake.

My aunt Miriam ran a cottage business in Oklahoma growing African Violets and fresh herbs. This recipe is adapted from one that I found in her handwritten kitchen notebook, dated July, 1943. Early popovers were often flavored with drippings from roasts or other ingredients, like the Yorkshire puddings made in England.

2 tablespoons butter, melted for brushing popover cups	¼ teaspoon salt
1½ cups whole milk	3 tablespoons minced fresh herbs, or 3 teaspoons dried (basil, dill, or tarragon)
3 large eggs	3 tablespoons freshly grated Parmesan cheese
1½ cups unbleached all-purpose flour	

PREP TIME: 15 MIN
BAKE TIME: 40 MIN

1. Preheat oven to 400°F. Brush six 3¼-inch muffin cups or heavy popover cups with the melted butter.

2. In a food processor or blender, or using an electric mixer, combine milk, eggs, flour, and salt. Process just until batter is smooth. With a spoon, stir in herbs and Parmesan cheese.

3. Ladle batter into prepared cups, filling up to ¼ inch below rims. Bake for 40 minutes, or until puffed and very well browned and firm to the touch. Remove from oven and immediately run a knife around edge of each popover to loosen. Invert to release. Serve immediately. (For extra-crisp popovers, see page 133.)

1 popover: 237 calories, 10 g protein, 10 g total fat (5.1 g saturated), 27 g carbohydrates, 248 mg sodium, 127 mg cholesterol, 1 g dietary fiber

WILD RICE HARVEST POPOVERS

MAKES 6 POPOVERS

Wild rice, harvested in the north woods of Minnesota's lake country, adds its distinctive, nutty flavor to these popovers. Long ago dubbed "rice" because it grows in water, wild rice is actually the seed of an annual marsh grass.

If I know that I'm making these delicious popovers, I plan to serve wild rice earlier in the week and make extra rice. Cooked wild rice will keep in the refrigerator for up to 5 days, and the small amount of red onion and garlic needed for this recipe will only take a couple of minutes to cook in the microwave.

3 tablespoons wild rice	1½ cups whole milk
3 tablespoons minced red onion	3 large eggs
1 garlic clove, minced	1½ cups unbleached all-purpose flour
1 cup water	¼ teaspoon salt
2 tablespoons butter, at room temperature for brushing popover cups	

1. Rinse wild rice in a strainer under running water. Drain. Combine rice, red onion, garlic, and water in a small, heavy saucepan. Bring to a boil over high heat. Cover, reduce heat, and simmer until rice is tender to the bite, about 55 minutes. Drain well and let cool. (You will have ½ cup of cooked rice.)

2. Preheat oven to 400°F. Brush six 3¼-inch muffin cups or heavy popover cups with the melted butter.

3. In a food processor or blender, or using an electric mixer, combine milk, eggs, flour, and salt. Process until batter is smooth. With a fork, lightly mash the cooked wild rice; stir into the batter.

4. Ladle batter into prepared cups, filling up to ¼ inch below rims. Bake for 40 minutes, or until puffed and very well browned and firm to the touch. Remove from oven and run a knife around edge of each popover to loosen. Invert to release. Serve hot. (For extra-crisp popovers, see below).

**PREP TIME:
1 HR
(15 MIN IF USING PRECOOKED RICE)

BAKE TIME:
40 MIN**

1 popover: 230 calories, 9 g protein, 9 g total fat (4.5 g saturated), 29 g carbohydrates, 190 mg sodium, 125 mg cholesterol, 1 g dietary fiber

EXTRA CRISPY POPOVERS

Popovers baked at 400°F will have a richly browned shell and fairly moist interior. For extra-crisp popovers, bake the popovers for 35 minutes. Quickly make a slit in the side of each popover with the tip of a sharp knife for the steam to escape and return to oven to bake for 5 to 10 minutes more.

CHOCOLATE CHIP SCONES

MAKES 16 SCONES

My grandmother made scones with oats and baked them on a griddle to serve with tea. Today, these Scottish quick breads are more often made with flour and baked in the oven.

These scones are good beyond belief when topped with Raspberry Butter.

3 cups unbleached all-purpose flour	½ cup (1 stick) cold butter, cut into 8 pieces
¼ cup sugar	3 large eggs
1 tablespoon baking powder	1 cup lowfat (1.5%) buttermilk
½ teaspoon baking soda	1 cup semisweet chocolate chips
½ teaspoon salt	

PREP TIME: 20 MIN
BAKE TIME: 12–15 MIN

1. Heat oven to 400°F. Lightly grease a baking sheet.
2. In a large bowl, sift together flour, sugar, baking powder, baking soda, and salt. Using a pastry blender or two knives, cut in butter until mixture resembles coarse crumbs. Set aside.
3. In a small bowl, whisk together eggs and buttermilk until frothy. Make a well in the center of flour mixture; pour in egg mixture and chocolate chips, stirring just until dry ingredients are moistened. Do not overmix.
4. Turn dough out onto a lightly floured work surface. Pat to 1-inch thickness. Cut into sixteen 2½-inch rounds, reusing scraps until all dough is used. Place 2 inches apart on prepared baking sheet.
5. Bake for 12 to 15 minutes, or until golden.

1 scone: 220 calories, 5 g protein, 10 g total fat (5.9 g saturated), 29 g carbohydrates, 286 mg sodium, 56 mg cholesterol, 1 g dietary fiber

RASPBERRY BUTTER

MAKES 1½ CUPS

PREP TIME: 10 MIN

1 cup fresh raspberries
½ cup (1 stick) unsalted butter, at room temperature
1 tablespoon sugar

1. Rinse raspberries; drain on paper towels.
2. In a small bowl, by hand, cream together the butter and sugar. Gently stir in raspberries, taking care not to mash the berries. Spoon into a small serving bowl. Cover and refrigerate for up to 4 days (do not freeze because the raspberries will become mushy). Let butter come to room temperature before serving.

1 tablespoon: 38 calories, 0 protein, 4 g total fat (2.4 g saturated), 1 g carbohydrates, 1 mg sodium, 10 mg cholesterol, 0 dietary fiber

DILL PARMESAN SCONES

MAKES 8 SCONES

A nice change from sweet scones, these are savory and just right to serve with a hearty soup or stew. Scones are much like biscuits, except they are usually richer with eggs.

1 cup unbleached all-purpose flour	½ cup freshly grated Parmesan cheese
¼ cup stone-ground cornmeal	3 tablespoons cold butter, cut into 3 pieces
½ tablespoon baking powder	1 large egg
½ teaspoon dried dill weed	½ cup whole milk
½ teaspoon salt	

PREP TIME: 15 MIN
BAKE TIME: 12–15 MIN

1. Preheat oven to 400°F. Lightly grease a large baking sheet or 9- or 10-inch shortbread mold (if using a mold, preheat in oven for 4 minutes).

2. In a large bowl, combine flour, cornmeal, baking powder, dill weed, salt, and Parmesan cheese. Using a pastry blender or two knives, cut in butter until mixture resembles coarse crumbs.

3. In a small bowl, whisk together egg and milk until frothy. Make a well in the center of flour mixture, pour in egg mixture, stirring just until dry ingredients are moistened. Do not overmix.

4. Form into a ball. Transfer to prepared baking sheet and pat into a 9-inch round, about 1-inch thick. Or, pat into a prepared, preheated shortbread mold.

5. If baking directly on the baking sheet, use a sharp knife to make score marks not quite all the way through as if you were cutting 8 wedges of pie. Bake for 15 to 18 minutes, until golden. Cut or break into 8 wedges before serving.

1 scone: 159 calories, 6 g protein, 8 g total fat (4.4 g saturated), 17 g carbohydrates, 401 mg sodium, 45 mg cholesterol, 1 g dietary fiber

DRIED CHERRY SCONES

MAKES 12 SCONES

During the summer, the bakery I use sells cherry scones that are cake-like and delicious, but quite expensive so I've tried to duplicate them, using dried cherries. If you don't have dried cherries, substitute dried apricots.

Like biscuits, dough for scones can be dropped from a spoon onto the baking sheet. They won't have the same perfectly round shape, but they'll taste every bit as good as scones that are rolled and cut out.

2 cups unbleached all-purpose flour	½ cup dried cherries
3 tablespoons firmly packed light brown sugar	1 cup heavy cream
1 tablespoon baking powder	2 large eggs
¾ teaspoon salt	1 teaspoon vanilla extract
¼ teaspoon ground cinnamon	1½ tablespoons granulated sugar,
3 tablespoons cold butter, cut in 3 pieces	for sprinkling

**PREP TIME:
15 MIN
BAKE TIME:
12–15 MIN**

1. Preheat oven to 400°F. Lightly grease a baking sheet.

2. In a large bowl, combine flour, light brown sugar, baking powder, salt, and cinnamon. Using a pastry blender or two knives, cut in butter until mixture resembles coarse crumbs. Stir in dried cherries.

3. In a small bowl, whisk together heavy cream, eggs, and vanilla extract. Make a well in the center of flour mixture. Pour in egg mixture, stirring just until dry ingredients are moistened. Do not overmix.

4. Drop the dough by heaping spoonfuls into 12 mounds onto prepared baking sheet. Sprinkle with granulated sugar. Bake for 12 to 15 minutes, until golden.

1 scone: 209 calories, 4 g protein, 11 g total fat (6.6 g saturated), 24 g carbohydrates, 304 mg sodium, 70 mg cholesteol, 1 g dietary fiber

PUMPKIN SCONES

MAKES 16 SCONES

You can also make these with cooked and mashed sweet potatoes or any of the winter squashes. Try these for dessert with fresh fruit.

4½ cups unbleached all-purpose flour
½ cup sugar
1 tablespoon baking powder
1 teaspoon salt
1 teaspoon ground cinnamon
½ teaspoon ground ginger
¼ teaspoon ground cloves
6 tablespoons (¾ stick) cold butter, cut into 6 pieces

5 large eggs
1 cup canned pumpkin or fresh pumpkin, cooked and mashed
½ cup whole milk
⅓ cup chopped, toasted pecans (see page 99)

CINNAMON TOPPING
¼ cup confectioners' sugar
1 teaspoon ground cinnamon

PREP TIME: 20 MIN
BAKE TIME: 12–14 MIN

1. Preheat oven to 350°F. Lightly grease a baking sheet.
2. In a large bowl, combine flour, sugar, baking powder, salt, and spices. Using a pastry blender or two knives, cut in butter until mixture resembles fine crumbs.
3. In another large bowl, whisk together eggs, pumpkin, and milk. Stir in pecans. Make a well in the center of the flour mixture. Pour in egg mixture, stirring just until dry ingredients are evenly moistened. Do not overmix.
4. Turn dough out onto a lightly floured work surface and pat or roll into a large rectangle, 1-inch thick. Using a sharp knife, cut into sixteen 2- x 3-inch diamonds. Place scones on prepared baking sheet, about 2 inches apart. Bake for 12 to 14 minutes, until golden.
5. **Prepare Cinnamon Topping:** While scones are baking, combine confectioner's sugar and cinnamon. When baked, transfer scones to a rack and immediately dust with sugar mixture. Serve hot or warm.

1 scone: 249 calories, 6 g protein, 8 g total fat (3.5 g saturated), 38 g carbohydrates, 294 mg sodium, 79 mg cholesterol, 2 g dietary fiber

SOURCES

MISSOURI DANDY PANTRY
(black walnuts)
414 North Street
Stockton, MO 65785
(800) 872-6879

SACO FOODS, INC.
(dry buttermilk)
6120 University Avenue
P.O. Box 620707
Middleton, WI 53562
(800) 373-7226

MAYTAG DAIRY FARMS
(Maytag Blue Cheese)
P.O. Box 806
Newton, IA 50208
(800) 247-2458

AMERICAN SPOON FOODS
(Michigan dried cherries and dried cranberries)
P.O. Box 566
Petoskey, MI 49770
(800) 222-5886

DYMPLE'S DELIGHT
(canned sweetened persimmon pulp)
Route 4, Box 53
Mitchell, IN 47446

MOZE'S GOURMET SPECIALTIES
(wild rice, dried cherries, and cranberries)
2701 Monroe Street
Madison, WI 53711
(800) 369-7423

INDEX